INSPIRING
CHOCOLATE

INSPIRING
CHOCOLATE

—— INVENTIVE RECIPES FROM
RENOWNED CHEFS

TEXT **CLAIRE PICHON**
PHOTOGRAPHY **MATTHIEU CELLARD**
STYLING **GARLONE BARDEL**

ABRAMS / NEW YORK

W eiss started with a story: the story of a man and his passion, but also the story of a town and especially, a very particular set of skills.

This is the story of Weiss. A name and an unmistakable signature forever linked to the art of indulgence. A House like no other, making chocolate for the finest confectioners and gourmet aficionados alike.

Since 1882, the year Eugène Weiss first set himself up as a pastry chef in Saint-Étienne, his little business has grown to be a French benchmark for excellence in fine chocolate making, producing a range of couverture chocolate, chocolate bars and other delights that are now sold all over the world.

But what strikes you about Weiss today is not so much its commercial success as its creative energy. A driving force fueled by unshakable core values and a fierce attachment to the Saint-Étienne coalfield, the place where it all began. Because the fact is that Weiss would not be Weiss without Saint-Étienne: the rollicking 19th century town that gave it birth. A town that flaunted its individuality, its privileged location off the beaten track in east-central France and its commitment to art and all things creative. The town that made Weiss chocolate in its own image.

Today, four decades later, at a time when authentic products true to their roots are finally making a comeback, Weiss has never been more modern. And it is this ability to deliver state-of-the-art performance without ever denying its roots that is perhaps Weiss' greatest achievement.

That, and its talent for producing superlative chocolate.

140 YEARS

OF

chocolate

STORY

Eugène, or where it all started

You can't miss him when you first visit Weiss. His picture extends across the entire width of the chocolate factory – a larger-than-life reminder of the man known to his employees as Monsieur Eugène. A man so full of ideas that he is still the heart and soul of Weiss in the 21st century, never mind that the last person who actually knew him retired more than 100 years ago.

ONCE UPON A TIME, IN ALSACE...

… a baby boy was born. He came into the world on 26 December 1858, in Ebersheim, the son of a farmer called Xavier Weiss and his homemaker wife, Elisabeth. They named him Eugène and he was the fifth of six children. He grew up in the straitened circumstances typical of his working-class background, the key event being the Franco-Prussian war. He was 12 in 1870 when Prussia invaded and annexed Alsace. Yet another change of flag for a land too rich and beautiful for its own good. As the war took its toll, poverty, instability and destruction followed, and migration became inevitable. Eugène was still very young at the time; but in 1875, the year of his seventeenth birthday, he formally renounced his Alsatian citizenship and said goodbye to his homeland.

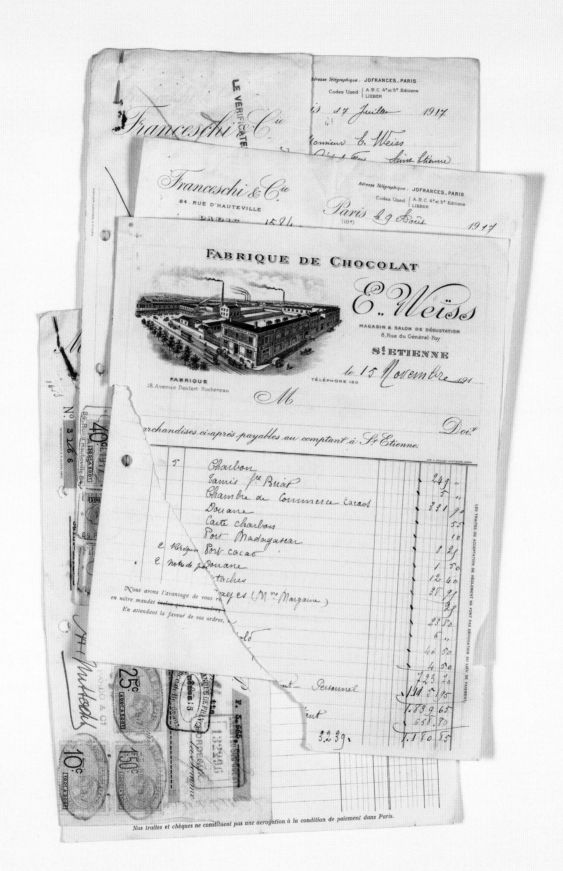

The historic Weiss boutique
on the Rue du Général-Foy
in Saint-Étienne – an enduring
symbol of elegance and good taste.

TRAVEL AND TRAINING

Like his brother Léon, Eugène left his native region and opted (maybe out of necessity) for a career in baker's confectionery. Geneva at the time being the chocolate and confectionery capital of the world, we can only guess that this is where the brothers headed to start their training. In truth, all we know for sure about their apprentice years is that Eugène became friends with Swiss-born Émile Gerbeaud and that Léon somehow left for England where he set himself up as a pastry chef and chocolatier. Eugène and Émile, for their part, chose to settle in Saint-Étienne.

HOME OF CHOCOLATE

If the Saint-Étienne coalfield may seem an odd choice for two aspiring chocolatiers, think again, because the town itself was famous back then as the home of French chocolate. Located on the banks of the River Loire, on one of the busiest rail junctions in France, Saint-Étienne was what we would now call a trade hub: a center for the free flow of goods and with them, imported products. Add to that, warehouses, the easy availability of labor and increasingly savvy manufacturers, and you can see what attracted chocolatiers to Saint-Étienne – among them Granetias, Escoffier, Pelletier, Pupier and Chocolat Coulois, the only brand still going strong today.

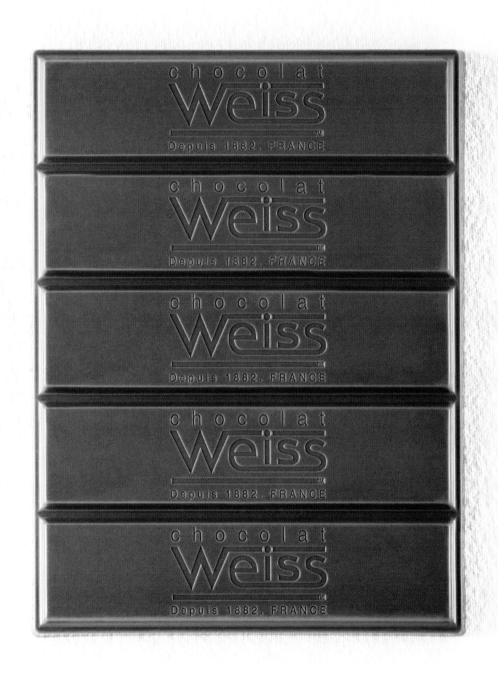

BIRTH OF A PATISSERIE DESTINED TO BECOME A CHOCOLATERIE

In 1879 Émile Gerbeaud bought a going concern in Saint-Étienne where he settled with his wife Esther – he the son and grandson of pastry chefs, she the daughter of a pastry chef and chocolate maker. We know that by 1881 Eugène and Émile were already working together. Meanwhile Henrik Kugler, the childless but soon-to-retire owner of the celebrated Kugler pastry shop in Budapest, was having trouble finding a worthy successor – someone who could live up to the reputation of one of the most venerated patisseries in Europe. So he sought the advice of his former Swiss master, who recommended Émile Gerbeaud. And just like that, everything changed. Gerbeaud surprised everyone by accepting the offer, placing his Saint-Étienne business in the hands of Eugène Weiss and moving to Hungary. The rest as they say is history: Café Gerbeaud became one of the sweetest success stories of the late 19th century. Practically an institution in Budapest, the café still stands today, nearly 150 years later, as a vibrant testament to gourmet excellence.

WEISS SPREADS HIS WINGS

The chocolate factory's well-preserved molds are a testament to careful product design.

Back in Saint-Étienne, Eugène took a leaf out of brother Léon's book and focused entirely on chocolate production, reckoning that what worked in England would work in France too. His intuition served him well. Weiss' success still hinges on the winning ideas he came up with more than a century ago: blending only top-grade cocoa beans; working with local artisans; developing innovative marketing tools (catalogues, for instance); and, of course, promoting the gourmet gift as a new dimension in the art of giving. A happy marriage with the lovely Eugénie Giroy produced two daughters, Marthe and Marcelle, and when Eugène retired in 1919 he handed the reins to his son-in-law, Albert Margaine, Marthe's husband. Sometime earlier, Albert had been joined by his brother Paul, who inherited the business after Albert's untimely death in 1925. Due to a bureaucratic blunder however, Paul's surname would forever be misspelled Margainne (not Margaine like his brother). Eugène himself continued to live life to the full until his own death in 1939.

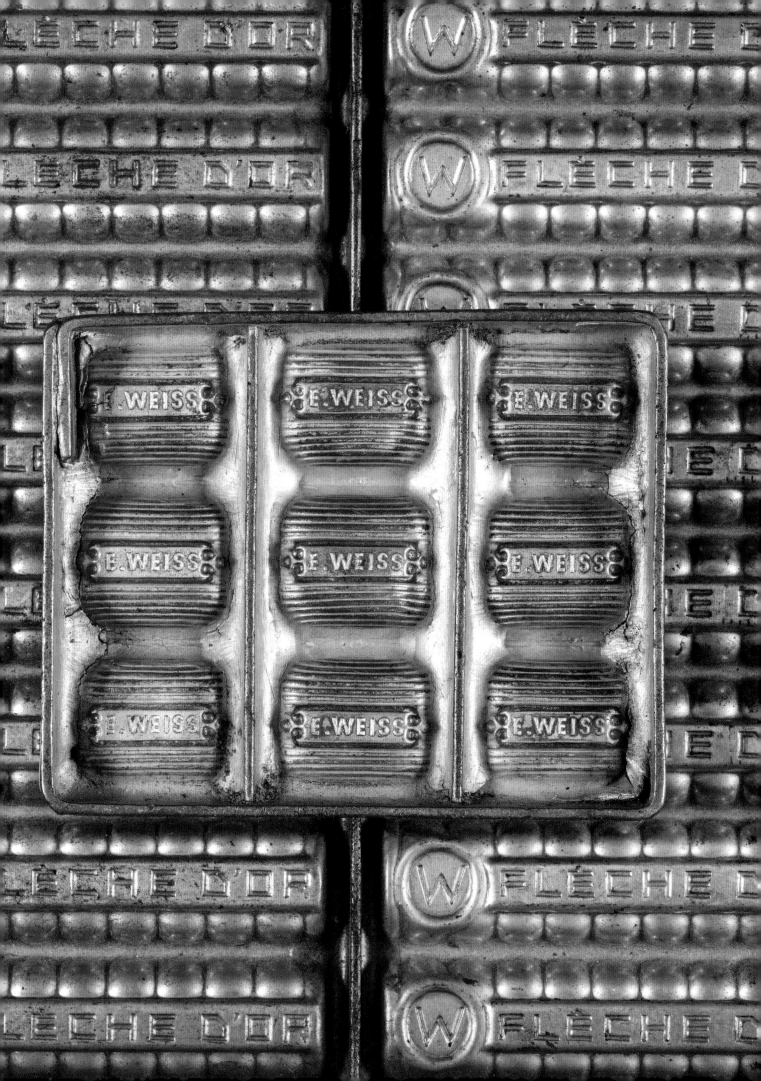

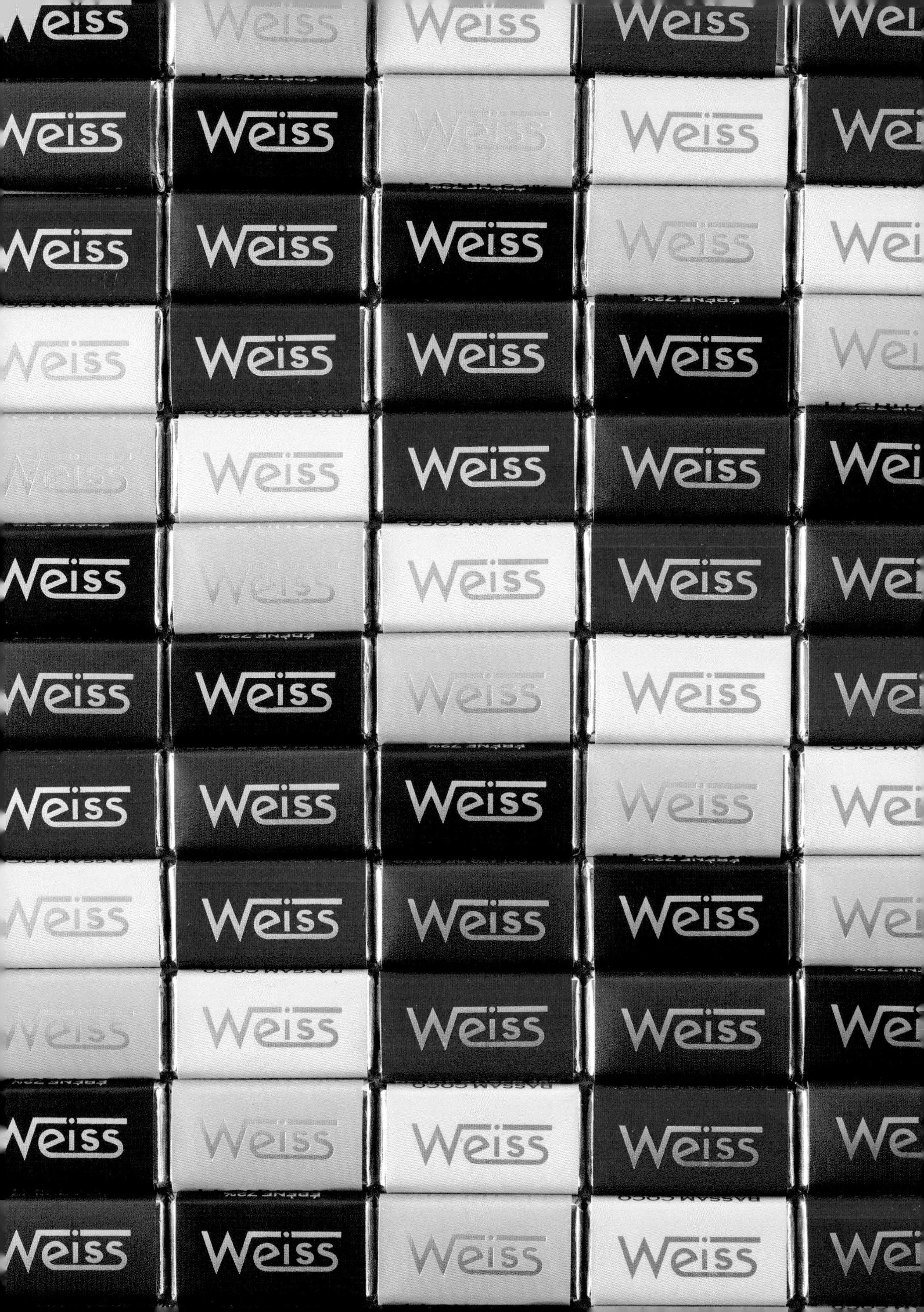
Weiss

The 20th century: from Eugène to the present day

Weiss' iconic "Napolitains" are still the best choice for anyone seeking a moment of stylish chocolate indulgence.

A STORY THAT SPANS THE CENTURIES

With Weiss already a well-established brand, the chocolate factory retained its original name when the Margainne family took over.

Its success was a tribute to Eugène Weiss' unstoppable drive – an impetus that propelled the business forward from the very beginning, marrying true craftsmanship with visionary leadership. The result was performance management, and an extraordinary capacity to innovate that endures to this day. Creativity informs everything that Weiss does.

Besides making very good chocolate from a careful blend of the very best beans, Eugène Weiss created an extremely versatile selection of offerings way ahead of their time (a chocolate specially made for diabetics, for instance). Many are still among Weiss' best sellers, whether his range of couverture chocolate for professional use or his irresistible array of sweets and chocolate bites – proof that well-made products always stand the test of time.

Success was not long in coming. Having made his name in the region, Eugène set out to win renown throughout the country, so in 1912 he published a mail-order catalogue. These days we think nothing of picking up the phone to place an order for chocolates; but back then distance-selling and food deliveries (by horse-drawn carriage!) were something totally unheard of.

In many ways, chocolate-making at Weiss has remained unchanged for more than a century – timeless skills speak for themselves!

It was a stroke of genius, not least because it chimed perfectly with another of his brilliant ideas: the art of giving. Before ever the concept of the customer experience became part of the marketing lexicon, Eugène Weiss understood that there is much more to giving chocolate than tasting pleasure alone. No matter how excellent his products, presentation mattered – so he took packaging to a whole new level (more about this later in the book), complete with poems and ditties specially composed by famous writers.

Paul Margainne and his descendants ensured the company's continued success in the 20th century, building on the founder's exceptional legacy of achievements. The name of Weiss remains a byword for luxury chocolate but also for a commitment to design and innovation that places this company at the forefront of contemporary trends in patisserie. Examples include Ébène and Acarigua couverture chocolate and, more recently, Anëo low-sugar white chocolate. Now part of Groupe Savencia together with other famous chocolate brands like Valrhona and La Maison du Chocolat, Weiss is better placed than ever to reach out to people everywhere and share its vision of chocolate as an art and a statement of good taste.

After 140 years of existence, the timeless codes of Weiss

Nearly a century and a half since the business was founded, Eugène Weiss remains more than ever the impetus behind everything it does. His thinking and his creative intuition inform and enrich every decision taken by the people who run the factory today.

ROOTED IN PLACE

Weiss is first and foremost a Saint-Étienne business – once you've understood that, you've basically understood it all. Promoting its beloved community far and wide is a daily preoccupation for this company that was awarded the Entreprise du Patrimoine Vivant label in 2014 in recognition of its exceptional French know-how. Growth for Weiss must reflect the spirit of the land that gave it birth – a vision it shares through its partnerships with other locally rooted entrepreneurs. All of its ribbons for instance are locally produced by uniquely skilled manufacturers with a global reputation.

140 YEARS OF CHOCOLATE STORY

A COMMITMENT TO ART
AND DESIGN

Weiss graphic design also expresses this sense of belonging and always has done. As a founding partner of the "Cité du Design de Saint-Étienne" design center, Weiss regularly works with the best budding talents in the business – graphic illustrators like Lucie Albon and Laure Lhuillier for instance. The results are partnerships that provide fertile ground for new ideas, whether new candy boxes celebrating the art of giving, or indulgent recipes for anything from imaginative twists on the Christmas Yule log to elegant plated desserts. No other chocolate maker takes artistic creativity as seriously as Chocolat Weiss.

A DARING TALENT
FOR BLENDING

Then of course, there is the art of crafting great chocolate. As the son of a vigneron, Eugène Weiss had an instinctive talent for blending – not grapes in his case, but different cocoa varieties, which he mixed together to create a rich and harmonious blend of flavors (or amalgams as they were known at the time). Eugène Weiss did for chocolate what famous noses did for perfume and famous cellarmasters did for Champagne: he created blends, exceptional blends that would set the tone for the Weiss signature style. Today it is Weiss chief pastry chef, Jonathan Chauve, and his team of chocolatiers who come up with the blends that make Weiss chocolate bars and couverture chocolate so successful. Examples range from the iconic, intensely chocolatey, Ébène to the whiter-than-white Anëo – an exercise in purity that reinvents the codes of pastry-making with white chocolate.

SKILLED
know-how

The art of bean-to-bar blending

Bean-to-bar : the process of making chocolate from fresh cocoa pods, as championed by Weiss and other craft chocolate makers who today more than ever deserve our admiration for their commitment to artisan production.

_____

There is no substitute for experience and expertise when it comes to selecting the best cocoa beans to make the best chocolate.

Cocoa beans, like all living things, possess different sensory attributes depending on the plantation and year of production. The chocolate maker may decide to focus on one dimension in particular by crafting a single-origin chocolate. Or they may decide to encompass all dimensions by crafting a multi-origin chocolate – a chocolate that, rather like a great perfume, plays on the unique flavor obtained by combining selected beans from several crus (growths). Therein lies the art of blending.

EXCLUSIVE EXPERTISE

Eugène Weiss took to his new life as a chocolate maker from the very beginning. A passion that shines through in his carefully recorded technical sheets that describe his couverture blends, each one as meticulously numbered as a luxury perfume.

Number 1 for instance brought together 10 crus from all over the world (from Java to Madagascar by way of the Equator) and contained "only" 42% sugar. Simpler blends, on the other hand, such as his five-estate couverture blend number 4, contained more than 50% sugar by mass. It took a truly formidable palate and flavor memory – not to mention infinite patience – to turn these into the unique recipes that remain Weiss' specialty today.

BOLD COMPOSITION

Over the years of course, Weiss has adapted its recipes to suit changing tastes – blends change because customer tastes change. But the method remains unchanged: you take carefully selected beans and you turn them into fine chocolate. And you do it with bravura what's more, aiming for a palate-rousing chocolate that is the very antithesis of bland. Every day Weiss' teams of blenders face the delicate task of balancing subtlety and approachability. Even though the House will occasionally release a single-origin chocolate (such as its deliciously fruity Li Chu, sourced exclusively from Vietnam), its core expertise lies in blending different types of chocolate.

Selection, blending and composition
– artistry in pursuit of the finest
chocolate takes work, intuitive thinking
and discerning taste buds.

SKILLED KNOW-HOW

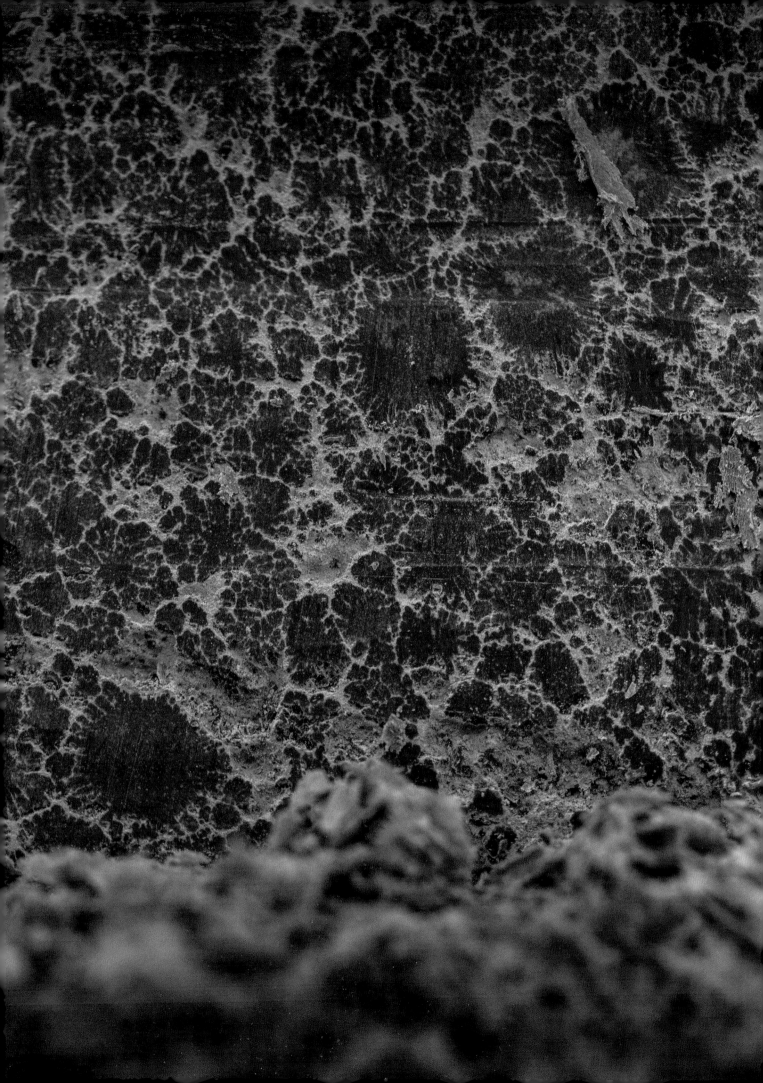

BLENDING EXPLAINED

Decoding three iconic compositions

DESCRIBED HERE ARE THREE KEYNOTE BLENDS THAT HELP TO EXPLAIN HOW WEISS' MASTER ARTISANS MANAGE TO DEVISE RECIPES THAT MEET THE EXPECTATIONS OF EVEN THEIR MOST DEMANDING CUSTOMERS, CRAFT CHOCOLATIERS AND AFICIONADOS OF CHOCOLATE BARS AND CANDY ALIKE.

— ÉBÈNE —
CHOCOLATEY INTENSITY

One taste tells you this is an unashamedly intense chocolate: top notes of cocoa supported by well-judged bitterness, with an irresistible toastiness that showcases the talents of the roaster without jeopardizing balance. No bells and whistles, just an uncompromisingly dark chocolate for dark chocolate lovers, based on a tried and tested recipe that is now part of the Weiss DNA. Available as a chocolate bar and in pistole form for melting and baking applications.

— CHOCOCÈPES —
CUSTOM-MADE CHOCOLATE

Chococèpes is a unique blend of cocoa beans and dried mushrooms, created in collaboration with French chef Régis Marcon. The result is a taste unlike anything you have ever tasted before: an unforgettable impression of earthiness, this time with the cocoa notes following on from the concentrated forest floor and umami flavors from the dried ceps. Not everyone's cup of tea certainly, but no less addictive even for people not normally fussed about chocolate — so be warned! This is a chocolate that perfectly exemplifies the high standards applied by Weiss' master blenders: talented artisans always pushing the limits of what's possible.

— ANËO —
THE QUEST FOR PURITY

For the uninitiated, Anëo is one of the couverture chocolates most sought after by chefs — as you might expect of a chocolate with a very unusual flavor profile that's been a hit with craft chocolate makers from the very beginning. This is a whiter than white, white chocolate (Anëo is Inuit for "snow"), with deliciously milky notes but a very understated sweetness for a white chocolate. Specially crafted by Weiss' R&D teams to meet the growing demand for chocolate that chimes with the times, Anëo is a shining testament to their talent for decoding new consumer behavior.

Chocolate-making and praline-making at Weiss

A high-quality cocoa mass begins with lovingly grown and carefully harvested cocoa beans.

Weiss Haut-Chocolat is the fruit of 140 years' experience that comes together in its chocolate-making teams. That's one hundred and forty years of meeting the challenges inherent in the science of chocolate, from the supply of cocoa to the packaging and distribution of chocolate bars, candy boxes and bags of chocolate pistoles.

CHOOSING TOP-QUALITY BEANS MATTERS

For the chocolate maker, cocoa supply is a complex process where every little detail counts, starting with the farming practices themselves, whether manual or mechanical. To ensure transparency, Weiss always sets out to buy directly from the producer through partnerships with local cooperatives known for their high ethical and environmental standards.

In Cameroon for instance, Weiss and enterprising grower Aristide Tchemtchoua work together as a team to produce fine-flavor cocoa in her home village of Nkog-Ekogo. Though very much in its infancy, the production of certified cocoa (as here by the Chocolatiers Engagés or "committed chocolatiers") is quite a departure from the intensively farmed cocoa for industrial use more typical of Cameroon production. The result is a virtuous circle where both sides benefit: the local producer because a higher price tag makes for a better livelihood; and the buyer because lovingly grown cocoa beans make for characterful chocolate with wonderfully complex aromas. A case in point is the 71% dark chocolate Mbô ("bean" in local parlance): yellow fruits on the nose, powerfully intense but deliciously rounded, and exclusively made from beans sourced from Aristide Tchemtchoua's plantation.

GLOBAL PARTNERSHIPS

Weiss works hard to develop strong personal relationships with growers throughout the world, preferably through direct buying to ensure supply chain visibility but also to create opportunities for new adventures.

Where direct buying isn't an option, Weiss works with trusted intermediaries who can be relied upon to buy beans that meet its exacting quality standards. The year 2021 marked the release of Weiss Li Chu chocolate: a delicate Grand Cru chocolate sourced through Weiss' intermediary partner, the Vietcacao association. As a member of uncompromising Swiss NGO Earthworm, Weiss is also actively committed to improving conditions in the most vulnerable parts of global chains.

Choice of producer matters all the more because of what happens after the cocoa pod has been removed from the tree: all of those inescapable but delicate stages executed on the cocoa plantation itself, affecting not only flavor but also food safety. Fermentation and drying are good examples, both being essential for flavor development and for the control of microbial growth in the cocoa bean. After 140 years in business, nobody knows better than Weiss just how important is the choice of producer when it comes to food safety.

CHOCOLATE METAMORPHOSIS
STAGE ONE

Back in France, Weiss takes delivery of carefully selected beans, all of them destined for the chocolate factory in Saint-Étienne. It is a point of pride with Weiss that all of its chocolate is made in France, and all of its couverture chocolate comes from the chocolate workshops in Saint-Étienne.

This is the place where Weiss' chocolate makers apply the methods bequeathed to them by Eugène and his successors: methods honed by years of practice in crafting chocolate that meets their expectations. A superlative chocolate – dependably excellent and always with that unmistakable note of intense roasting that is Weiss' stock-in-trade.

CHOCOLATE-MAKING
THE WEISS WAY

Roasting is the first essential step in chocolate-making: think of it as an obligatory rite of passage in the life of a cocoa bean. The roasting process is tailored to suit each cru ("growth"), applying just enough heat for just enough time to bring out the aromas expected by chocolatiers. One by one, the sacks of beans are emptied into a large tank where they swirl around until the heat penetrates to the core, releasing a fabulously intense bouquet that hits you as you enter the roasting room. Once smelled, never forgotten. Next the beans are given a good shaking: fed into a cocoa breaker that removes the outer shell of the bean then breaks the inner flesh into small pieces called "cocoa nibs" that vary in size depending on the program.

The third stage is grinding: feeding the nibs between two rollers that reduce them to tiny particles. This is also the stage when cocoa butter comes on the scene – a lead character in cocoa production that is squeezed out of the cocoa nibs under the pressure of the rollers, turning the cocoa particles into an incredibly pungent paste rich in fatty acids.

This paste is then transferred to a kneader where it is mixed with sugar and sometimes milk powder depending on the recipe. Once this cocoa mass is fully kneaded, it undergoes additional grinding to break the cocoa particles into ever-finer fragments or flakes – the smaller the size, the creamier the chocolate and the longer the flavors linger in the mouth.

The next stage is conching, a term largely unfamiliar to the layperson that describes what is probably one of the most pivotal steps in the chocolate-making process. It involves stirring and aerating the chocolate mass, a combination of mechanical action and air input that is essential to achieve a silky-smooth texture while also reducing acidity. How long to conch depends on the result the master chocolatier has in mind – the process can last anywhere from a few hours to two days.

The final stage is tempering: the process of heating and cooling the chocolate following a precise temperature curve (up to 30 degrees Celsius/86 degrees Fahrenheit) to give it a glossy finish plus that combination of snap and smoothness expected by aficionados.

The chocolate is now ready for molding into bars and pistoles or incorporating into other recipes.

PRALINE: ANOTHER WEISS SPECIALTY

The almonds and hazelnuts that go into Weiss praline are as rigorously selected as the cocoa beans used to make its high-quality couverture chocolate.

Chocolate has always enjoyed a privileged relationship with praline. We need only look at the way praline is made to realize that the process is strikingly similar. Roasting, grinding and even conching form part of the praline lexicon, which like chocolate is about transforming solids into a smooth paste – with equally delicious results.

So it is hardly surprising to learn that Weiss' connection with praline goes back a very long time. All the way back to 1882 in fact, the year Eugène Weiss founded his business and determined to make a mouthwatering caramelized nut butter (aka praline) of his own. And not just any praline, but praline with credentials made exclusively from the finest ingredients. Piedmont hazelnuts for instance, awarded protected status in 1993 for their intensely nutty flavor, featured in Weiss praline decades before they won PGI ranking. The almonds meanwhile are of the Marcona and Valencia varieties and come from small orchards in Spain where they, like all of their nutty counterparts, are harvested at peak ripeness by growers who allow plants to grow at their own pace and in their own time.

The steps involved in praline-making
are similar in many ways to the chocolate
making process.

To make praline, Weiss' maîtres praliniers (master praline makers) mix together nuts and sugar then heat the mixture slowly,
spreading it evenly as they go. Their movements are slow
and deliberate, aiming for a very gradual roasting that brings
out the nutty flavors. Little by little, the sugar coats the nuts
and then melts, leaving a clear glossy caramel whose warmth
somehow transcends the taste of the hazelnuts and almonds.
This mixture is left to rest, then ground to varying degrees
of fineness, gradually acquiring a paste-like consistency that
becomes smoother, silkier and distinctly less granular as the
grinding progresses. Sugar and nut content vary with the type
of praline, to offer craft confectioners an array of taste experiences and intensities – a Weiss specialty honed over centuries
of experience in the making of world-class confectionery.

The art of
gift giving

There is more
to a great gift
than fine chocolate
alone …

WEISS SPECIALTIES

A portion of Weiss production is destined for professional use by leading pastry chefs, bakers, chocolatiers, ice-cream makers and other adventurous cooks in culinary labs everywhere. The rest is molded into bars or used to make those gourmet delicacies for which Weiss first became famous 140 years ago. Among them are luscious chocolate and praline confections originally crafted by Eugène Weiss himself and still made today, with quite as much care, by the confectioners and chocolatiers now following in his footsteps. Hence their appeal as gifts for connoisseurs of subtle but sensational sweet experiences.

A SELECTION OF ICONIC WEISS DELICACIES

— NAPOLITAINS —

The perfect mouthful of chocolatey indulgence, made for giving, easy to carry around and virtually unbreakable. The ideal way to sample Weiss signature blends at any time of day, whether enjoyed with coffee or nibbled on the go.

— NOUGASTELLE AND NOUGAMANDINE —

Invented by Paul Margainne in 1930, these ravishing little bites were his take on the cobblestones of France's *route bleue* — the famous Nationale 7 highway known to French holidaymakers of the '50s and '60s as the "road to the sun". Combining crunchy nougatine with creamy praline, they have served as a celebration of the art of French confectionery for nearly a century.

— ORANGETTES —

Candied orange peel enveloped in dark chocolate strewn with shards of nougatine — an irresistible Weiss confection that makes the perfect gift.

— LANGUES DE CHAT AND CHOC'INES —

Weiss artisans thought hard about what makes a good tasting sample and they came up with these thin but intensely chocolatey cats' tongues. Available in a pure chocolate version (Weiss langues de chat) or studded with nuts and dried fruit (Weiss Choc'ines), this is the ideal gift for the discerning connoisseur.

— BÂTON CRÈME —

Chocolate on the outside, luscious vanilla cream on the inside, Weiss bâtons crème bring you the taste of nostalgia ...

Wrapper and ribbon: Weiss signature packaging

Ever since the chocolate factory first opened in 1882, product packaging has always held great importance for Weiss. Looking back through old catalogues, you have to marvel at the creativity of Weiss employees back then – all those women and men who went to such pains to design confectionery boxes that spoke to their customers' imaginations. Delicate, ingenious designs, with no two alike, each box exquisitely decorated and impeccably judged in terms of materials, typeface and shape. Chocolate-box scenes of famous French roads appear alongside charming poems and little stories penned by famous writers. Many of these boxes display the words *Le plaisir d'offrir* (the pleasure of giving). All of them reveal a conspicuous talent for keeping up with the spirit and design trends of the times.

The chocolate assortments themselves go by names that conjure up images of journeys, presented in Persian, Egyptian and Roman-style gift boxes. Some make more obvious allusions to gift-giving occasions, whether a baptism (the panier Baptême and the Marraine or godmother assortment), the onset of winter (Premiers Froids gift box) or even an unwelcome birthday (the tactfully named Très Jeune selection).

The 1950s saw a move to more daring times and with them, candy boxes spelling out a rather clearer message – Je plais ("people find me attractive"), Votre joie ("for your delight"), Fol espoir ("mad hopes") and the rather more enigmatic Malgré tout ("despite everything").

But most striking of all is the sheer luxury of the containers themselves, especially those dating from the first half of the 20th century: marquetry candy boxes, porcelain bonbonnières, wicker candy baskets, Italian ceramic candy dishes and even crystal candy jars signed Baccarat, Daum and Gallé. More modest budgets could choose from a range of fancy cardboard boxes, all of them quite as charmingly decorated.

The art of ribbon-making
still survives in the Saint-Étienne region.
For Weiss, which has always taken
the greatest care with its packaging,
the idea of doing without ribbons
is simply inconceivable.

This taste for beautifully executed packaging designs was ever a hallmark of Weiss, which views product packaging as a showcase for local arts and crafts. The ribbons used to decorate its gift boxes are a case in point. All of them come from ribbon weavers in the Loire, a region famous for its ribbon-making skills, and are so important to Weiss that the ramp leading from the factory to the Boutique des Ateliers (gift store) is specially designed to resemble the flowing, graceful ribbons that decorate its boxes. For Weiss, every detail counts.

INVENTIVE
RECIPES FROM

RENOWNED
Chefs

CONTENTS

W eiss has specialized in chocolate and praline products for the consumer market, together with culinary products for cooking labs and professional kitchens for 140 years now. This dual specialty is largely unknown among chocolatiers and places Weiss in a unique position as a purveyor of gourmet goods to the French and international market.

On the professional side, building rapport with customers is of pivotal importance to Weiss. Restaurant chefs, artisan bakers, pastry chefs in the best hotels and coffee-shops – all readily testify to the quality of their day-to-day relationship with the Weiss teams. Chocolate is a sensory but also a technological product, with tastes and techniques that evolve every day. By working together, culinary creatives and chocolatiers can work miracles.

Weiss cannot imagine working any other way. Many of the sweet inventions in its product catalogue sprang from close working relationships with the best chefs – acting on their inspiration to bring out the personality behind their delectable desserts. A prime example is Michel and Sébastien Bras' world-beating "coulant au chocolat" – made with Weiss chocolate from the outset. For Weiss, the pursuit of creativity and modernity often means breaking the rules, as when working with Régis Marcon on the genesis of his chocolatey tribute to mushrooms, Chococèpe. Teaming up with master baker Raoul Maeder meanwhile produced Les Sublimes – chocolate chips that keep their shape and structure even with prolonged cooking. Weiss history, like French gastronomy in general, is filled with such examples of fruitful culinary collaboration.

Weiss has always been a business on a human scale. A proximity-based business, with a real spirit of service and that proven expertise in its field that counts for so much in the world of craftspeople and artisans. Hence their many delicious contributions to this book, each one a story of chocolate adventuring with the best in the business – Weiss. World-famous chefs, incredible pastry chefs, dedicated artisans: revealed in the following pages is their vision of the world of chocolate according to Weiss …

Chef and proprietor of Le Neuvième Art restaurant, Lyon

For these coconut caramel chocolate truffles, I chose Kacinkoa chocolate for its character and its strong presence in the mouth, precisely what one is looking for in a truffle.

CHOCOLATE TRUFFLES

with coconut caramel and coconut ice cream served in a coconut shell

SERVES 6

Preparation time : 1 hour
Resting time : 24 hours
Cooking time : 5 minutes
Freezing time : 4 hours

6 half-sphere silicone molds,
2 ½ in (6 cm) in diameter
6 silicone disk molds, 2 ½ in (6 cm)
in diameter and ½ in (1 cm) deep

Coconut ice cream

2 tablespoons (25 g)
superfine sugar
3 ½ oz (90 g) atomized glucose
1 pinch (2 g) stabilizer for ice cream
3 ½ tablespoons (50 ml) UHT milk
1 cup (260 ml) water
1 lb 2 oz (500 g) Sicoly®
coconut cream

Truffles

1 sheet (2 g) leaf gelatin
2 oz (60 g) egg yolk (about 3 yolks)
2 oz (60 g) whole egg
(about 1 ¼ eggs)
⅓ cup (2 ½ oz/75 g) sugar
4 teaspoons (20 ml) water
6 ¾ oz (190 g) Weiss
Kacinkoa 85 % dark chocolate
½ cup (125 ml) UHT
whipping cream
1 cup (250 ml) whipped cream

Preparing the coconut ice cream

Mix the sugar, glucose, and stabilizer together. In a small saucepan, heat the milk and water to 122 °F (50 °C). Add the glucose mixture and heat everything to 183 °F (84 °C). Pour over the coconut cream and let rest in the refrigerator for 24 hours. Pour the mixture into a Pacojet® bowl and place in the freezer.

Preparing the truffles

Soak the gelatin in cold water for 10 minutes. Put the egg yolks, eggs, sugar, and water in the bowl of a small stand mixer and heat everything in a bain-marie to 176 °F (80 °C). Whisk until thickened, then continue whisking until cold.

Meanwhile, melt the chocolate to 95 °F (35 °C). Heat the cream, squeeze out the gelatin leaf, and add. Mix and pour over the melted chocolate. Mix everything lightly together, add the whisked egg mixture, and then the whipped cream. Transfer to the half-sphere 2 ½-in (6-cm) molds, smooth the surface flat, then freeze.

Continuation of the recipe **CHOCOLATE TRUFFLES**

Coconut disks

4 ½ oz (130 g) egg white
(about 4 ¼ whites)
¾ cup (5 ¼ oz/150 g) sugar
8 oz (220g) grated coconut
1 ¾ oz (50 g) apple compote

Coconut caramel

⅔ cup (160 ml) coconut milk
7 oz (200 g) coconut purée
3 ½ oz (100 g) glucose syrup
7 oz (200 g) white fondant
3 ½ oz (100 g) Isomalt
2 teaspoons (10 ml) white rum

For assembling and finishing

Weiss 100 % cocoa powder
6 empty half shells of fresh
coconuts, kept in the freezer
Flesh of ½ fresh coconut removed
from the shell, for decoration

Preparing the coconut disks

Using a spatula, mix all the ingredients together in a mixing bowl until evenly combined. Press into the silicone disk molds, packing the mixture in tightly. Freeze.

Preparing the coconut caramel

Heat the coconut milk and coconut purée in a small saucepan. In another saucepan, prepare a caramel with the glucose syrup, fondant, and Isomalt. When the caramel turns a blonde color, lower the cooking temperature by adding the milk and coconut purée. Add the rum, mix in, leave to cool, and refrigerate.

Assembling and finishing

Unmold the coconut disks and immediately cook them for 5 minutes in a 400 °F (210 °C/Gas Mark 6) oven; the shreds of grated coconut must be colored. Leave to cool, then unmold a half-sphere of truffle onto each coconut disk. Keep at room temperature. Just before serving, dust with cocoa powder and place a coconut disk in the center of each half coconut shell. Blend the caramel with a hand-held blender to make it smooth and shiny.

For decoration, cut thin slices of fresh coconut using a mandolin and blanch them in water with a little sugar added. Drain. Fill the half coconut shells with the coconut ice cream from the Pacojet and decorate with the thin coconut slices. Serve the truffles accompanied with the ice cream and the coconut caramel.

Jonathan Chauve

Pastry chef and Master Chocolatier at Weiss

This complex dessert is an absolute delight as well as an occasion. The Anëo white chocolate is powdered and then dusted hot over the same very cold chocolate, giving the dome its velvety texture. On top, there is a slight gradation of dark Ceïba chocolate and, in the fluffy mousse, the elegant notes of yellow fruits can be detected.

COMET

SERVES 6

Preparation time :
1 hour 30 minutes
Chilling time : 7 hours
Freezing time : a few minutes
Cooking time : 1 hour 20 minutes

6 silicone half-spheres molds,
2 ½ in (6 cm) in diameter
6 silicone half-spheres molds,
2 ¾ in (7 cm) in diameter

Chocolate shortcrust pastry
Generous ½ cup (3 ½ oz/90 g)
brown rice flour
3 tablespoons (22 g)
Weiss cocoa powder
⅓ teaspoon (1.5 g) guar gum
½ cup (1 ½ oz/42 g)
powdered almonds
Pinch (1 g) salt
3 tablespoons (44 ml) coconut oil
2 tablespoons (30 ml) water

Chocolate pavlova
3 ½ oz (100 g) egg white
(about 3 ½ whites)
Scant ½ cup (3 oz/82.5 g)
superfine sugar
1 tablespoon (¼ oz/7.5 g)
Weiss cocoa powder
Generous ½ cup (3 oz/82.5 g)
confectioners' sugar
Vegetable oil for the molds

Kumquat and golden Inca berry marmalade
7 oz (200 g) kumquats
1 ¾ oz (50 g) dried golden
Inca berries
1 vanilla bean
⅔ cup (4 ½ oz/133 g)
superfine sugar
1 teaspoon (5 g) glucose
syrup DE40

Fluffy Ceïba 64 % dark chocolate mousse
1 teaspoon (4 g) powdered gelatin
200 Bloom
5 teaspoons (24 ml) water
7 oz (210 g) Weiss Ceïba
64 % dark chocolate
2 ½ oz (71 g) egg white
(about 2 whites + 2 teaspoons)
⅓ cup (2 ½ oz/71 g)
granulated sugar
1 ½ oz (43 g) trimoline
1 oz (28 g) glucose syrup DE40
Generous 1 cup (266 ml) whole milk
Generous 1 cup (266 ml)
whipped cream

Namelaka hazelnut praline Piedmont IGP
½ teaspoon (2 g) powdered gelatin
200 Bloom
2 ½ teaspoons (12 ml) water
3 ½ tablespoons (50 ml)
whipping cream
4 ¾ tablespoons (70 ml) whole milk
12 oz (350 g) Weiss 60–40 hazelnut
praline from Piedmont IGP
¾ cup (175 ml) whipping cream,
well chilled

Praline Piedmont IGP condiment
5 ¼ oz (150 g) Weiss
60–40 hazelnut praline
from Piedmont IGP
Hazelnut oil
Small pinch (0.5 g) fleur de sel
Kumquat zest
Green cardamom

Preparing the chocolate shortcrust pastry

Mix all the dry ingredients together in the bowl of a stand mixer fitted with the paddle beater. Melt the coconut oil to 77 °F (25 °C) and add it to the bowl, followed by the water, beating until you have a smooth dough. Immediately roll the dough to a thickness of $\frac{1}{16}$ in (2 mm) between two sheets of parchment paper. Chill in the refrigerator for a few minutes then cut into star shapes. Bake them in a fan oven preheated to 300 °F (150 °C/Gas Mark 2) for 15–20 minutes.

Preparing the chocolate pavlova

Heat the egg whites with the superfine sugar in a bain-marie to 122 °F (50 °C), then whisk them to stiff peaks in a stand mixer fitted with the whisk, keeping the motor running until the whites are cold. Sift the cocoa and confectioners' sugar over the whisked whites and fold in to make a smooth, shiny meringue. Transfer the meringue to a pastry bag. Lightly oil the rounded part of the 2 ½-in (6-cm) silicone half-spheres and pipe in domes of meringue. Bake for about 30 minutes in a fan oven preheated to 212 °F (100 °C/Gas on lowest setting); the inside of the meringue domes must remain soft. Set aside in a dry place until assembling.

Preparing the kumquat and golden Inca berry marmalade

Plunge the kumquats into a saucepan of boiling water. Bring back to a boil, drain immediately, and rinse the kumquats under cold water. Repeat this process three or four times to remove the bitterness from the citrus fruits and to soften them. Add the Inca berries and blend to a purée but taking care to leave a few pieces. Add the vanilla bean, split with the seeds scraped, and sugar and bring to a simmer. Let simmer over gentle heat until the mixture is thick and candied. Check the Brix reading using a refractometer (+ or − 65 °Brix), then add the glucose syrup. Cool the mixture rapidly in the freezer, then store at 39 °F (4 °C) until assembling.

Preparing the fluffy Ceïba 64 % dark chocolate mousse

Soak the gelatin in the water to rehydrate it. Melt the chocolate in a bain-marie. In the bowl of a stand mixer, whisk the egg whites with the sugar, trimoline, and glucose syrup. Heat the mixture to 104 °F (40 °C), then whisk to a meringue. Bring the milk to a boil, melt the gelatin in it, and pour the mixture over the chocolate, blending to an emulsion using a hand-held blender.

When the temperature of the mixture drops to 118 °F (48 °C), fold in a little of the whipped cream using a flexible spatula, followed by the meringue, and finally lightly fold in the rest of the whipped cream. Cover the surface of the mousse with plastic wrap and set aside for about 1 hour in the refrigerator.

Preparing the namelaka hazelnut praline Piedmont IGP

Rehydrate the gelatin with the water. Bring the first quantity of whipping cream and the milk to a boil. Melt the gelatin in it, then pour the mixture over the hazelnut praline. Blend with a hand-held blender, add the well-chilled cream, and blend again, then set aside for at least 6 hours at 39 °F (4 °C).

Preparing the praline Piedmont IGP condiment

Mix the praline with enough hazelnut oil until it has a slightly runny consistency and add the crushed fleur de sel. Add a little finely grated kumquat zest and a pinch of freshly ground green cardamom. If necessary, add hazelnut oil to achieve the desired consistency, then transfer the condiment to a paper piping cone.

Recipe photograph, page 71. **69**

Continuation of the recipe **COMET**

Leopard half-spheres

10 ½ oz (300 g) Weiss Anëo 34 % white chocolate

Yellow spray

2 oz (60 g) Weiss cocoa butter
5 oz (140 g) Weiss Anëo 34 % white chocolate
Yellow food coloring

Chocolate spray

1 ¾ oz (50 g) Weiss cocoa butter
5 ½ oz (150 g) Weiss Ceïba 64 % dark chocolate

For assembling and finishing

Trimoline in a paper piping cone
Hazelnut "envelopes" (skins from blanching whole hazelnuts)
Edible gold leaf
Cubes of fresh kumquat
Limon Cress Koppert®

Preparing the leopard half-spheres

Temper the Anëo chocolate keeping to the following temperatures: 113 °F (45 °C), then 79 °F (26 °C), then 84 °F (29 °C). Spread the chocolate into the 2 ¾-in (7-cm) silicone half-spheres in as thin a layer as possible, about ¹⁄₁₆ in (1.5 mm). When the chocolate begins to set in the molds, use a toothpick to pierce holes to create "leopard spots" of different sizes. Let set in the refrigerator (at 59 °F/ 15 °C), until unmolding.

Melt the ingredients for the two sprays separately. Add yellow food coloring to the white chocolate mixture to tint it your desired shade.

Unmold the leopard half-spheres and place them in the freezer for a few minutes. Using chocolate spray guns, first spray them with the yellow mixture and then with a little of the dark chocolate mixture. Let set.

Assembling and finishing

Grate the base of each pavlova to create a flat surface so they will be stable when placed on serving plates. Stick hazelnut "envelopes" around the pavlovas using the piping cone filled with trimoline. Using a teaspoon, carefully fill the inside of each pavlova with kumquat marmalade.

Place a pavlova in the center of each serving plate. Pipe a drop of praline condiment over, then cover the center with fluffy Ceïba mousse, place the star in chocolate shortcrust pastry then pipe a dome of Ceïba mousse using a pastry bag fitted with a ¾-in (20-mm) plain tip.

Pipe a dot of namelaka hazelnut praline in the center of the mousse.

Add fresh kumquat cubes and a few drops of praline condiment. Finish by placing a leopard half-sphere on top and a few leaves of limon cress.

Galaxie milk chocolate allows me to make a light ganache, the sweetness of which brings out the delicate flavor of the lentils that come from my native Haute-Loire.

ANICIA CUSHION

with chocolate and lentil ganache

SERVES 4

Preparation time : 40 minutes
Resting time : 12 hours 30 minutes
Cooking time : 2 minutes

Cushions
1 ¾ oz (50 g) spinach purée
Generous ¾ cup (3 ½ oz/100 g) all-purpose flour
1 oz (25 g) lentil flour
⅛ oz (3.5 g) fresh yeast
¾ teaspoon (3 g) salt

Ganache
Scant ½ cup (100 ml) whipping cream, 30 % fat + ½ cup (120 ml) at the end
¼ oz (7 g) liquid glucose
¼ oz (7 g) trimoline
1 ¾ oz (50 g) Weiss Galaxie 41 % milk chocolate, chopped
3 ½ oz (100 g) mashed lentils flavored with ground Chinese star anise

Preparing the cushions
(make the day before)

Mix the spinach purée with 2 tablespoons plus 2 teaspoons (40 ml) water and press through cheesecloth to obtain 3 tablespoons (45 ml) of spinach juice. In a mixing bowl, combine the flours, yeast, salt, and spinach juice. Knead everything together quickly without overworking the dough. Cover with plastic wrap and let rest for 12 hours in the refrigerator.

Roll out the dough thinly, dusting the work surface with as little flour as possible. Let rest for 15 minutes, then turn the dough over and let it rest for another 15 minutes.

Place a baking sheet in a fan oven, preheated to 475 °F (220 °C/Gas Mark 9). Cut the dough into 2 ½-in (6-cm) squares and place on the preheated baking sheet. Leave for 2 minutes to puff up.

Preparing the ganache
(make the day before)

Bring the scant ½ cup (100 ml) cream, the liquid glucose, and trimoline to a boil. Pour onto the chocolate off the heat. Add the mashed lentils, blend with a hand-held blender, then add the ½ cup (120 ml) cream. Refrigerate for 12 hours.

Assembling and finishing

Whisk the ganache to lighten it. Spoon it into a pastry bag fitted with a small plain tip, pierce each cushion with the tip, and fill the cushions with the lentil ganache. Serve 3 or 4 cushions per person.

Morgane Raimbaud

Pastry chef at the Alliance restaurant, Paris

I chose Santarém chocolate for its smokiness, which combines perfectly with the spiciness of Madagascan pepper, and accentuates the bitterness of the cocoa.

CHOCOLATE *with maple syrup and pecan nuts*
BRIOCHE PERDUE

SERVES 6

Preparation time : 2 hours
Resting and chilling time : 2 hours
Rising time : 2 hours
Cooking time : 1 hour

1 set of 7 teardrop cookie cutters ("balloon" shape) graduated from 1 to 7 by size

Chocolate brioche
3 ½ cups (15 oz/425 g) flour
⅓ cup (1 ½ oz/44 g) Weiss cocoa powder
¼ cup (1 ¾ oz/50 g) superfine sugar
1 ½ teaspoons (7 g) fine salt
½ cup (1 ¾ oz/50 g) powdered pecans
½ oz (15 g) fresh yeast
5 ¼ oz (150 g) whole egg (about 3 eggs)
⅔ cup (160 ml) whole milk
7 oz (200 g) butter, diced, at room temperature

Cocoa imbibing mixture
1 cup (250 ml) milk
1 cup (250 ml) whipping cream
3 tablespoons (⅔ oz/20 g) Weiss cocoa powder
7 oz (200 g) egg yolk (about 10 yolks)
⅓ cup (2 oz/60 g) superfine sugar

Maple syrup ice cream
2 cups (500 ml) milk
1 cup (250 ml) whipping cream
Voatsiperifery pepper (according to personal taste)
½ teaspoon (4 g) Stab 2000 (stabilizer for ice cream)
1 ¾ tablespoons (⅔ oz/20 g) superfine sugar
9 oz (250 g) maple syrup
4 ¼ oz (120 g) egg yolk (about 6 ½ yolks)

Chocolate and pepper crémeux
1 teaspoon (5 g) powdered fish gelatin
1 tablespoon + 2 teaspoons (25 ml) water
½ cup (125 ml) milk
½ cup (125 ml) whipping cream
½ teaspoon (2 g) voatsiperifery pepper
4 ¼ oz (120 g) Weiss Santarém 65 % dark chocolate
1 ¾ oz (50 g) egg yolk (about 3 yolks)
2 tablespoons (1 oz/25 g) superfine sugar

Preparing the chocolate brioche

Sift the flour with the cocoa. Place the sugar, salt, powdered pecans, and yeast (keeping this away from the salt), in the bowl of a stand mixer fitted with the dough hook. Mix briefly, then incorporate the eggs and the milk. Knead on speed 4 for 10 minutes, then add the diced butter. Knead for 20 minutes until the dough is very elastic and comes away from the sides of the mixer bowl. Shape the dough into a ball and let rise for 1 hour at room temperature in a container covered with plastic wrap. Knead the dough briefly to burst air bubbles inside it and let rest for 1 hour in the refrigerator, covered in plastic wrap. Preheat the oven to 325 °F (160 °C/ Gas Mark 3). Press the dough into a medium-size rimmed baking tray and let rise almost to the top of the tray. Bake in the oven for 35 minutes, then let cool. Cut the brioche horizontally into a layer about 1 ¼ in (3 cm) deep. Cut out 6 shapes from it using size 6 of the set of teardrop cookie cutters (the cutters are graduated from 1, the smallest, to 7, the largest). Set aside.

Preparing the cocoa imbibing mixture

Blend all the ingredients together. Set aside for imbibing the brioche before assembling.

Preparing the maple syrup ice cream

Heat the milk and cream with the pepper. Mix the stabilizer with the sugar, add, and bring to a boil. Cover and let infuse for 30 minutes, then strain through a fine-mesh sieve. Add the maple syrup and egg yolks, mix, then add the hot liquid. Cook, stirring constantly, until thickened, as for making a crème anglaise. Emulsify using a hand-held blender, then let cool and churn in an ice cream or sorbet maker.

Preparing the chocolate and pepper crémeux

Soak the powdered gelatin in the water until rehydrated. Weigh out ⅔ oz (18 g). Bring the milk, cream, and pepper to a boil. Take off the heat, cover, and let infuse for 30 minutes. Melt the chocolate in a bain-marie. Whisk the egg yolks and sugar together until they whiten, add the hot liquid, and cook until thickened, as for making a crème anglaise. Add the ⅔ oz (18 g) rehydrated gelatin, mix, and pour over the melted chocolate. Emulsify using a hand-held blender. Keep in the refrigerator.

Recipe photograph, page 77.

75

Continuation of the recipe **CHOCOLATE BRIOCHE PERDUE**

Pecan and chocolate shortbread

1 ½ cups (6 ½ oz/184 g) flour

4 ½ oz (132 g) pecans, ground to a fine powder

⅔ cup (3 ½ oz/90 g) confectioners' sugar, sifted

¼ cup (1 oz/30 g) Weiss cocoa powder, sifted

Pinch (1 g) fleur de sel

6 oz (165 g) butter

1 oz (25 g) egg yolk (about 1 ¼ yolks)

Chocolate tuiles

1 ¾ oz (50 g) butter

1 ¾ oz (50 g) egg white (about 1 ¾ whites)

⅓ cup (1 ¾ oz/50 g) confectioners' sugar

Scant ½ cup (1 ¾ oz/50 g) all-purpose flour

1 ½ tablespoons (⅓ oz/10 g) Weiss cocoa powder

Powdered pecan nuts

For finishing

Pecan nut powder and cocoa powder, for dusting

Purple oxalis leaves

Pecan nut splinters

Freshly ground voatsiperifery pepper

Preparing the pecan and chocolate shortbread

Beat all the ingredients, except the egg yolks, in the bowl of a stand mixer fitted with the paddle beater. Continue beating until you have an evenly textured sandy mixture, then add the egg yolks and mix to make a smooth dough. Shape the dough into a ball and roll it between two sheets of parchment paper to a thickness of ⅛ in (3 mm). Let rest for 1 hour in the refrigerator. Cut out 6 small teardrops using the cookie cutters to sit the ice cream on, and another 6 that are wider and perforated to be placed on the brioche. Bake between two Silpain® baking mats in a 330 °F (165 °C/Gas Mark 3) oven for 12 minutes.

Preparing the chocolate tuiles

Melt the butter, then mix it with the other ingredients. Spread the mixture over a Silpain® baking mat using an angled spatula. Bake in a 325 °F (160 °C/Gas Mark 3) oven for 8 minutes. As soon as they are removed from the oven, mold the tuiles by hand into attractive curved shapes.

Assembling and finishing

Imbibe the brioche shapes with the cocoa liquid, then toast them for 1 minute on each side in a very hot skillet. Spoon most of the crémeux into a pastry bag fitted with a Saint-Honoré tip, reserving a little. Using an oval stencil and an angled spatula, spread a little of the reserved chocolate crémeux over the center of each serving plate. Dust with pecan powder. Also dust cocoa powder in a teardrop shape using a stencil placed on each plate, for decoration.

Place the brioches on the plates, cover with a large shortbread shape, and pipe crémeux in the center of the shortbread. Place a smaller shortbread shape next to it to serve as a base for a small quenelle of maple syrup ice cream. Decorate with a few oxalis leaves and pecan nut splinters. Place a large and a small quenelle of ice cream on the shortbread shapes.

Top the quenelles with the cocoa tuiles and grind two turns of voatsiperifery pepper over each dessert.

Morgane Raimbaud

Pastry chef at the Alliance restaurant, Paris

For this dessert, I wanted a chocolate that was quite conservative, but was also indulgent. With its biscuit notes, Galaxie milk chocolate coats the palate and mellows the power of the aniseed.

PEANUT

star anise and yogurt desserts

SERVES 6

Preparation time :
1 hour 30 minutes
Cooking time : 40 minutes
Resting time : 30 minutes

Peanut praline

7 ½ oz (212 g) salted peanuts
¾ cup (5 ¼ oz/150 g)
superfine sugar

Whipped peanut ganache

1 teaspoon (5 g) powdered fish
gelatin
1 tablespoon + 2 teaspoons
(25 ml) water
3 oz (75 g) Weiss Galaxie 41 %
milk chocolate
Scant 1 cup (225 ml)
whipping cream
1 ½ oz (45 g) peanut praline
⅔ cup (150 ml) whipping cream,
well chilled

Peanut lace cookies

¼ cup (1 ¼ oz/33 g)
confectioners' sugar
2 tablespoons (½ oz/16 g)
all-purpose flour
1 ½ oz (40 g) egg white
(about 1 ½ whites)
¾ cup (173 ml) water
½ oz (16 g) butter
Peanut splinters

Yogurt and star anise sorbet

1 cup + 2 tablespoons
(285 ml) water
3 tablespoons (45 ml) pastis
1 pod (8 g) star anise
½ cup (3 ¾ oz/105 g)
superfine sugar
¾ teaspoon (6 g) stabilizer
for ice cream
7 oz (200 g) Greek yogurt
2 tablespoons (30 ml) lemon juice

Lemon and pastis gel

2 tablespoons + 2 teaspoons
(40 ml) lemon juice
2 tablespoons + ½ teaspoon
(32 ml) pastis
Scant ⅔ cup (140 ml) water
¾ teaspoon (1.2 g) agar-agar
Ground star anise
⅔ teaspoon (2 g) rehydrated
gelatin (set aside from the step
for making the ganache)

Recipe photograph, page 80.

Preparing the peanut praline

Roast the peanuts on a baking sheet in a 330 °F (165 °C/Gas Mark 3) oven for 16 minutes. Cook the sugar to a light brown caramel and add the peanuts. Let cool slightly, then reduce to a paste using a Thermomix.

Preparing the whipped peanut ganache

Soak the powdered gelatin in the water to rehydrate it, then set aside ½ oz (15 g). Keep the rest for making the lemon and pastis gel. Melt the milk chocolate. Bring the first quantity of cream to a boil, adding the ½ oz (15 g) rehydrated gelatin. Add the melted chocolate and emulsify with a hand-held blender. Add the peanut praline, blending constantly, then the well-chilled cream. Keep in the refrigerator.

Preparing the peanut lace cookies

Sift the confectioners' sugar and the flour together and add the egg whites. Bring the water and butter to a boil and add them to the mixture, whisking constantly. Pour the mixture onto a Silpain® baking mat and sprinkle with peanut splinters. Bake in a 330 °F (165 °C/Gas Mark 3) oven for 15 minutes. Let cool, then break the lace cookie sheet into pieces. Return the pieces to the oven between two silicone baking mats for 2 minutes. When they come out of the oven, mold them into curved shapes. Set aside.

Preparing the yogurt and star anise sorbet

Heat the water, pastis, star anise, and half the sugar together. Mix the stabilizer with the rest of the sugar and add. Bring to a boil, take off the heat, cover, and let infuse for 30 minutes. Let the syrup cool, strain it through a fine-mesh sieve, then blend in a Thermomix with the yogurt and lemon juice. Churn to make a sorbet. Keep in the freezer.

Preparing the lemon and pastis gel

Bring the first five ingredients to a boil. Take off the heat and add the reserved rehydrated gelatin. Let stiffen at room temperature, then chill well in the refrigerator. Blend, then transfer to a pastry bag and keep chilled.

Continuation of the recipe **PEANUT STAR ANISE**

Caramelized peanuts

⅓ cup (2 ¼ oz/65 g)
superfine sugar
Generous ¾ cup (20 ml) water
4 ¼ oz (125 g) peanuts
¼ oz (7 g) butter
Fleur de sel

Gluten-free peanut sponge

5 ¼ oz (150 g) whole egg
(about 3 eggs)
1 oz (30 g) egg yolk
(about 1 ½ yolks)
4 ½ oz (130 g) peanuts,
ground to a powder
1 ¼ cups (6 oz/160 g)
confectioners' sugar
½ oz (12 g) cornstarch

Pastis and lemon yogurt

3 ½ oz (100 g) Greek yogurt
4 teaspoons (20 ml) pastis
1 teaspoon (5 ml) lemon juice
Ground star anise

For finishing

Finely ground peanut powder
Caramelized peanut splinters
Atsina Cress Koppert®
Ground star anise

Preparing the caramelized peanuts

Make a hard-ball syrup (about 257 °F/125 °C) with the sugar and water, add the peanuts, and heat, mixing until the peanuts are coated in cooked sugar, then let caramelize. Take off the heat, add the butter to separate the peanuts, then add a pinch of fleur de sel. Spread the mixture over a baking sheet, let cool, then cut into splinters.

Preparing the gluten-free peanut sponge

Place the ingredients in the bowl of a stand mixer and beat them together on high speed. Spread the mixture over a baking sheet lined with parchment paper and bake in a 340 °F (170 °C/ Gas Mark 3) oven for 24 minutes. Using a cookie cutter, cut out shapes (in the photograph the sponge is cut using a bespoke cutter, but you can use a rectangular cookie cutter). Allow 2 pieces of sponge for each serving.

Preparing the pastis and lemon yogurt

Combine all the ingredients in a mixing bowl, then transfer to a pastry bag, and keep chilled.

Assembling and finishing

Using an angled spatula, spread the ganache over 6 serving plates. Dust with peanut powder.

Arrange the different elements on each plate so they form a mirror image as in the photograph: 2 sponge pieces, 2 bands of piped ganache on each sponge piece, 1 line of praline, then 1 line of lemon and pastis gel.

Arrange the peanut splinters and a few sprigs of Atsina Cress on top. Pipe a few dots of lemon and pastis gel and pastis and lemon yogurt around the sponge pieces.

Place a quenelle of yogurt and star anise sorbet on each, followed by a peanut lace cookie. Dust each serving with ground star anise.

Chef at the restaurants Le Suquet, Laguiole, and La Halle aux Grains, Paris

I chose Ceïba dark chocolate as its exotic notes of wood and spice blend beautifully with the green cardamom. Its length in the mouth and slightly sweet flavor is another asset.

COCOA NIB NOUGATINE MILLE-FEUILLE

with cardamom milk mousse and grand cru Dominican Republic chocolate sorbet

SERVES 6

Preparation time :
1 hour 30 minutes
Cooking time : 20 minutes
Maturation time : 24 hours

Ceïba sorbet
½ cup (3 ½ oz/100 g)
superfine sugar
2 ½ oz (70 g) atomized glucose
1 oz (30 g) stabilizer for sorbets
(Stab Prosorbet)
2 ¾ cups (640 ml) mineral water
6 oz (160 g) Weiss Ceïba
64 % dark chocolate, chopped
1 oz (30 g) glucose syrup

Cardamom milk mousse
2 sheets (4 g) leaf gelatin
1 ¼ oz (35 g) green cardamom pods
Scant ¼ cup (55 ml)
whipping cream, 35 % fat
12 oz (350 g) fromage blanc
Generous ¾ cup (200 ml) whipping
cream, 35 % fat
Scant ½ cup (3 ½ oz/90 g)
superfine sugar

Preparing the Ceïba sorbet

Mix the sugar, atomized glucose, and stabilizer together. Heat the water and when the temperature reaches 104 °F (40 °C), add the sugar mixture. Bring to a boil and pour over the chocolate and glucose syrup. Blend until evenly combined with a hand-held blender. Cool the mixture quickly in a blast chiller, then let it mature for 24 hours in the refrigerator. Strain through a fine-mesh sieve, then churn in a sorbet maker. Store in the freezer.

Preparing the cardamom milk mousse

Soak the gelatin in cold water. Grind the cardamom pods.

Bring 3 tablespoons (50 ml) of the cream and the cardamom to a boil and let infuse for 20 minutes. Strain through a fine-mesh sieve and add a little more cream to bring it back to its initial weight. Add the squeezed-out gelatin to the cream, pour the mixture over the fromage blanc, and mix until combined. Using an electric beater, whip the generous ¾ cup (200 ml) whipping cream, stiffening it with the sugar, but keep the consistency soft.

Fold the whipped cream into the fromage blanc and keep in the refrigerator.

Chocolate sauce

2 tablespoons (300 ml)
mineral water

2 ½ teaspoons (10 g)
superfine sugar

6 oz (160 g) Weiss Ceïba
64 % dark chocolate, chopped

Pinch (0.5 g) fleur de sel, crushed

Cocoa nib nougatine

10 ½ oz (300 g) Weiss cocoa nibs

1 ½ cups (10 ½ oz/300 g)
superfine sugar

1 teaspoon (5 g) pectin NH

Scant ½ cup (100 ml) milk

9 oz (250 g) softened butter

3 ½ oz (100 g) glucose syrup

For finishing

Green cardamom pods

Weiss cocoa nibs

Hot chocolate, to serve

Preparing the chocolate sauce

Bring the water and sugar to a boil and pour it over the chocolate in three equal quantities, mixing after each addition of water. Blend using a hand-held blender to emulsify the mixture and make it smooth. Add the fleur de sel and keep in the refrigerator in a sous vide bag.

Preparing the cocoa nib nougatine

Grind the cocoa nibs. Mix the sugar and pectin together.

Heat the milk, butter, and glucose syrup to 122 °F (50 °C). Add the sugar and pectin mixture and cook to 223 °F (106 °C). Add the cocoa nibs. Pour the mixture over a sheet of parchment paper and spread out with a spatula. Cover with a second sheet of parchment paper and roll out as thinly as possible. Freeze until solid. Bake in a 340 °F (170 °C/Gas Mark 3) oven for 15–20 minutes, then cut into 24 rectangles each measuring 1 ½ x 2 ¾ in (4 x 7 cm).

Assembling and finishing

Put the cardamom pods and cocoa nibs in a pepper mill. Heat the chocolate sauce. Spoon the cardamom mousse into a pastry bag fitted with a plain ½-in (14-mm) tip. Pipe two logs of mousse on 18 of the nougatine rectangles and assemble in three layers with a plain nougatine rectangle on top. Place the millefeuilles on their side in the center of 6 serving plates and top with a quenelle of sorbet. Grind green cardamom and cocoa nibs from the pepper mill on the side of each plate and serve with the chocolate sauce.

Régis Marcon

Chef at the Maisons Marcon, Saint-Bonnet-le-Froid

For this dessert, which combines several different textures and chocolate elements, 64 % Li Chu chocolate with its particularly fruity flavor, seemed to us the best match for the aroma and the challenge of pairing it with the roasted chicory root.

CHOCOLATE EXQUISITE *with roasted chicory root*

SERVES 4

Preparation time : 2 hours
Resting time : 28 hours
Freezing time : 4 hours
Cooking time : 57 minutes

Coffee granita
10 cups of espresso coffee
5 teaspoons (20 g) granulated sugar

Roasted chicory root crème brûlée
3 cups (750 ml) whipping cream
1 cup (250 ml) milk
1 ½ oz (45 g) roasted chicory root
8 ½ oz (240 g) egg yolk
(about 12 yolks)
1 cup (6 ½ oz/180 g) sugar

Whipped ganache
6 ¾ oz (188 g) Weiss Li Chu
64 % dark chocolate
Scant 1 cup (225 ml) whipping cream
1 oz (25 g) glucose syrup
1 oz (25 g) trimoline
1 ¾ cups (450 ml) whipping cream,
well chilled

Chocolate Sacher sponge
15 oz (430 g) almond paste 50 %
⅔ cup (4 ½ oz/130 g) superfine sugar
+ ¼ cup (1 ¾ oz/50 g) for whisking
the egg whites
7 ½ oz (210 g) egg yolk (about 10 ½ yolks)
5 ¼ oz (150 g) whole egg (about 3 eggs)
9 oz (250 g) egg white (about
8 ½ whites)
3 ½ oz (100 g) Weiss 100 % pure
cocoa paste
4 oz (100 g) butter
Scant ½ cup (1 ¾ oz/50 g)
Weiss cocoa powder
1 cup (3 ½ oz/100 g) cake flour (T45)

Chocolate sheets
5 ¼ oz (150 g) Weiss Li Chu
64 % dark chocolate

Preparing the coffee granita
(make the day before)

Mix the coffee and granulated sugar together. Freeze for at least 4 hours.

Preparing the roasted chicory root crème brûlée
(start the day before)

A day ahead, bring the cream and milk to a boil with the roasted chicory root. Take off the heat, cover the saucepan with plastic wrap, and keep in the refrigerator for 24 hours.

The next day, whisk the egg yolks and sugar together until they whiten. Whisk in the roasted chicory root-infused cream and milk. Strain through a fine-mesh sieve, then pour the mixture into a shallow pan or baking tray. Cook in a preheated 185 °F (85 °C/Gas on lowest setting) fan oven for 45 minutes.

Preparing the whipped ganache
(can be made the day before)

Chop the chocolate. Bring the cream, the glucose syrup, and trimoline to a boil and pour over the chocolate, stirring to combine. Emulsify using a hand-held blender, then chill the ganache in a covered container for at least 4 hours. You can prepare the ganache to this stage the day before making the recipe.

Preparing the chocolate Sacher sponge

In the bowl of a stand mixer, beat the almond paste with the superfine sugar. Mix in the egg yolks one by one, then the whole eggs, and continue to beat the batter until it reaches the ribbon stage. In a separate bowl, whisk the egg whites to firm peaks, adding the remaining sugar a little at a time.

Melt the cocoa paste with the butter. Sift the cocoa powder and flour together. Add the cocoa paste and butter mixture to the almond paste, stir in the sifted dry ingredients, and then fold in the whisked egg whites using a flexible spatula. Spread the mixture over a baking sheet lined with parchment paper and bake in a 350–400 °F (180–200 °C/Gas Mark 4–6) oven for 12 minutes. Let cool.

Preparing the chocolate sheets

Melt the chocolate in a bain-marie. Temper the chocolate (see the tempering instructions in the Chocolate Bites Perfumed with Tansy recipe, following page). Spread it over an acetate sheet and let set. Cut the chocolate into 8 rectangular sheets measuring 1 ½ x 4 in (4 x 10 cm) and keep them in a cool place for half a day.

Assembling and finishing

In a stand mixer, beat the 1 ¾ cups (450 ml) well-chilled cream into the chilled ganache. Transfer the ganache to a pastry bag fitted with a plain tip. Cut the chocolate Sacher sponge into four 1 ½ x 4-in (4 x 10-cm) rectangular blocks and place them on 4 serving plates. Pipe two parallel lines of ganache down the long sides of each sponge rectangle. Fill the middle with roasted chicory root crème brûlée and place a chocolate sheet on top. Pipe two more lines of ganache down the long sides of the chocolate sheets. Scrape a spoon over the surface of the granita to shave off crystals. Spoon them between the two piped lines of ganache, then cover with a second chocolate sheet.

Régis Marcon

Chef at the Maisons Marcon, Saint-Bonnet-le-Froid

We chose Mahoë 76 % as not only is it a chocolate with character and contains very little sugar, it also combines perfectly with the intriguing perfume of tansy.

CHOCOLATE *with tansy*
BITES PERFUMED

SERVES 6

Preparation time : 2 hours
Resting time : 7 hours
Cooking time : 15 minutes

Chocolate genoise
½ cup (2 ½ oz/65 g)
all-purpose flour
Generous ½ cup (2 ½ oz/65 g)
Weiss cocoa powder
Scant 1 cup (4 ½ oz/125 g)
cornstarch
7 oz (200 g) egg yolk
(about 10 yolks)
12 ½ oz (360 g) egg white
(about 12 whites)
1 cup (7 oz/200 g) superfine sugar

Whipped ganache with tansy
Generous ¾ cup (200 ml)
whipping cream
10 fresh tansy leaves
7 oz (200 g) Weiss Mahoë
76 % dark chocolate
1 oz (25 g) glucose syrup
1 oz (25 g) trimoline
Generous 1 ¾ cups (450 ml)
whipped cream

Chocolate disks
7 oz (200 g) Weiss Li Chu
64 % dark chocolate

Feuillantine praline
3 oz (75 g) Weiss Chococèpes
42 % milk chocolate with ceps
15 oz (425 g) Weiss praline
4 ½ oz (125 g) crepes dentelle
cookies, crumbled

Pears
4 Williams (Bartlett) pears
Butter
Lemon juice

Pear sorbet
Scant ½ cup (100 ml) water
⅔ oz (20 g) glucose syrup
2 ½ tablespoons (1 oz/30 g)
superfine sugar
⅛ teaspoon (1 g) stabilizer
for ice cream
1 tablespoon (15 ml) lemon juice
9 oz (250 g) pear pulp

Chocolate sauce
3 ½ oz (100 g) syrup at 30 °Baume
⅔ cup (150 ml) whipping cream
4 teaspoons (20 ml) water
3 tablespoons (⅔ oz/20 g)
Weiss cocoa powder
3 ½ oz (100 g) Weiss Galaxie
67 % dark chocolate, chopped

Preparing the chocolate genoise

Preheat the oven to 400 °F (200 °C/ Gas Mark 6). Sift the flour, cocoa powder, and cornstarch together. Whisk the egg yolks until they whiten. In a separate bowl, whisk the egg whites to firm peaks with the sugar, gently fold in the whisked egg yolks, then fold in the sifted ingredients. Spread the batter over a 16 x 24-in (40 x 60-cm) baking sheet lined with parchment paper and bake in the oven for 10 minutes. Let cool, then cut into rounds 1 ¼ in and 1 ½ in (3 and 4 cm) in diameter using cookie cutters (both sizes will be used on each serving plate).

Preparing the whipped ganache with tansy

Bring the whipping cream to a boil, add the tansy leaves, cover, and let infuse for 2–3 hours.

Melt the chocolate in a bain-marie.

Mix the infused cream with the glucose syrup and trimoline, bring to a boil again, and strain through a fine-mesh sieve over the melted chocolate. Mix well and let cool to 113 °F (45 °C). Fold in the whipped cream using a flexible spatula and keep in the refrigerator.

Preparing the chocolate disks

Melt the chocolate in a bain-marie until it reaches a temperature of 113 °F (45 °C). Stand the base of the container in cold water and stir the chocolate until the temperature drops to 82 °F (28 °C). Return the chocolate to the bain-marie and raise the temperature to 90 °F (32 °C). The chocolate is now tempered. Spread it over a baking sheet in a very thin layer, ¹⁄₁₆ in (1–2 mm) thick. Cut the chocolate into disks 1 ¼–1 ½ in (3–4 cm) in diameter using a cookie cutter, let set, then reserve.

Preparing the feuillantine praline

Melt the chocolate in a bain-marie, add the praline and crumbled crepes dentelle cookies. Spread the mixture over a baking sheet in a layer ¹⁄₁₆ in (1–2 mm) thick, then chill. Cut into rounds 1 ¼ and 1 ½ in (3 and 4 cm) in diameter using cookie cutters.

Preparing the pears

Peel and core the pears. Cut them into ¼-in (5-mm) cubes and sauté in a skillet over high heat with a knob of butter and a few drops of lemon juice until they start to soften (about 5 minutes). Set aside.

Preparing the pear sorbet

Make a syrup by bringing the water and glucose syrup to a boil. Mix the sugar with the stabilizer and add. Boil for 1 minute, add the lemon juice, and then the pear pulp. Let cool, then mature for 4 hours in the refrigerator. Churn in an ice cream or sorbet maker. Keep in the freezer.

Preparing the chocolate sauce

Bring the syrup, whipping cream, and water to a boil. Whisk in the cocoa powder and bring back to a boil. Pour the mixture over the chocolate, mixing well. Strain through a fine-mesh sieve and let chill.

Assembling and finishing

Spoon the ganache into a pastry bag fitted with a plain tip.

Reheat the chocolate sauce.

Assemble the desserts in layers as follows: chocolate genoise, feuillantine praline, piped ganache, and finally the diced pears. Place a chocolate disk on top, serve with the chocolate sauce, and the pear sorbet on the side.

Recipe photograph, page 91.

89

This chocolate adventure with the Weiss company began a long time ago and we have remained faithful to it since the beginning. We entrusted them with making our specialty, ceps praline, in order to improve it and produce it on a more regular basis. It is a blend of ceps praline and Ceïba Ghana milk chocolate, the whole containing 42 % cocoa solids.

CHOCOCÈPES CHIPS

SERVES 8

Preparation time : 1 hour
Resting time : 7 hours
Cooking time : 8 minutes

Chocolate genoise

½ cup (2 ½ oz/65 g) all-purpose flour
Generous ½ cup (2 ½ oz/65 g) Weiss cocoa powder
Scant 1 cup (4 ½ oz/125 g) cornstarch
7 oz (200 g) egg yolk (about 10 yolks)
12 ½ oz (360 g) egg white (about 12 whites)
1 cup (7 oz/200 g) superfine sugar

Chococèpes ganache

5 ½ tablespoons (85 ml) milk
5 ½ tablespoons (85 ml) water
⅙ oz (5 g) dried ceps, ground to a powder
7 oz (200 g) Weiss Chococèpes 42 % milk chocolate with ceps, chopped
1 ¼ oz (35 g) Weiss Mahoë 76 % dark chocolate, chopped
2 oz (55 g) Weiss hazelnut paste
Generous 2 cups (550 ml) whipping cream, well chilled

Lace cookies

½ cup (125 ml) water
4 ¼ oz (120 g) melted butter
7 oz (200 g) egg white (about 7 whites)
1 ⅔ cups (7 ¾ oz/220 g) confectioners' sugar, sifted
1 cup (4 ½ oz/125 g) flour
1 ½ teaspoons (7 g) salt

For finishing

Weiss Mahoë 76 % dark chocolate
Powdered ceps
Fresh ceps (or brown button mushrooms) cut into thin slices

Preparing the chocolate genoise

Preheat the oven to 400 °F (200 °C/ Gas Mark 6). Sift the flour, cocoa powder, and cornstarch together. Whisk the egg yolks until they whiten. In a separate bowl, whisk the egg whites to firm peaks with the sugar, gently fold in the whisked egg yolks, then fold in the sifted ingredients. Spread the batter over a 16 x 24-in (40 x 60-cm) baking sheet lined with parchment paper and bake in the oven for 10 minutes. Let cool.

Preparing the Chococèpes ganache

Bring the milk and water to a boil with the powdered ceps. Cover and let infuse for 1 hour.

Place the chopped chocolates and the hazelnut paste in a bowl. Strain the infused liquid through a fine-mesh sieve, bring it to a simmer, and pour it over the chocolates and hazelnut paste. Using a hand-held blender, emulsify the mixture and add the chilled cream. Keep in the refrigerator for half a day, covered with plastic wrap pressed over the surface of the ganache.

Preparing the lace cookies

Preheat the oven to 350 °F (180 °C/ Gas Mark 4). Using a hand-held blender, mix the water and melted butter together. Add the remaining ingredients and blend until completely smooth. Spread over a Silpat® baking mat, bake in the oven for 7 minutes, reversing the baking mat halfway, and finish baking at 325–340 °F (160–170 °C/ Gas Mark 3). Let cool, then cut into irregularly shaped fragments that are roughly triangular.

Assembling and finishing

Whip the well-chilled ganache with an electric beater and transfer it to a pastry bag fitted with a plain tip.

Temper the Mahoë chocolate (see the tempering instructions in the Chocolate Bites Perfumed with Tansy recipe, page 88) and spoon the chocolate into a paper piping cone. Pipe fine patterns around the edges of the serving plates for decoration. Cut disks of genoise 1 ¼ in (3 cm) in diameter using a round cookie cutter, place on the serving plates, and pipe the Chococèpes ganache over them. Cover with the lace cookie fragments, dust with powdered ceps, and finish each plate with a few mushroom slices.

Grégory Doyen

Travelling pâtissier and consultant to GD Sweet Concept

Ceïba, my favorite milk chocolate, has a strong cocoa flavor with hints of roasted coffee beans, which complement the cinnamon and bananas perfectly. After baking, the texture of the Sublime 29 % chocolate chips in a cake is superb. As for dark Galaxie, it is a classic that is liked everywhere, making it perfect for ganaches and chocolate decorations.

BANANA BREAD

**SERVES 6
(MAKES 2 CAKES)**

Preparation time :
1 hour 30 minutes
Resting time : 1 hour (for the raisins), 24 hours (for the ganaches)
Cooking time : 40 minutes

2 rectangular loaf pans measuring
6 ¼ × 3 × 3 in (16 × 7.6 × 7.5 cm)
Pastry bag fitted with a ribbon piping tip 104K

Banana bread batter
Generous ½ cup (3 ½ oz/100 g) golden raisins
6 ripe bananas
2 tablespoons + 1 teaspoon (40 ml) lemon juice
Scant 3 cups (12 ¾ oz/360 g) all-purpose flour
3 ¼ teaspoons (12 g) baking powder
⅓ teaspoon (5 g) baking soda
4 ¼ oz (120 g) butter
3 tablespoons (50 ml) grape seed oil
6 ½ oz (180 g) whole egg (about 3 ½ eggs)
1 ¾ cups (9 oz/250 g) light brown cane sugar
1 ⅓ cups (4 ½ oz/130 g) almond powder
½ teaspoon (2 g) ground cinnamon
5 ¼ oz (150 g) mascarpone
1 ¾ oz (50 g) Weiss Sublime
29 % milk chocolate chips

Chocolate ganache with cinnamon milk
1 ¾ sheets (3.6 g) leaf gelatin
⅔ cup (160 ml) + scant 1 ¼ cups (290 ml) whipping cream (used as separate quantities)
½ teaspoon (2 g) ground cinnamon
10 ¼ oz (290 g) Weiss Ceïba
42 % milk chocolate, chopped
5 ¼ oz (150 g) Weiss pecan praline

Dark chocolate ganache
Generous 1 ½ cups (380 ml) whipping cream
1 ½ oz (40 g) vanilla paste
1 oz (30 g) glucose syrup
2 ½ oz (70 g) trimoline
2 ¾ oz (70 g) butter
13 oz (370 g) Weiss Galaxie
64 % dark chocolate, chopped

Milk chocolate coating
1 lb 6 oz (625 g) Weiss Ceïba
42 % milk chocolate
½ cup (125 ml) grape seed oil
1 ¾ oz (50 g) Weiss pecan praline
⅓ cup (2 ¾ oz/75 g) pecan nuts, roasted and chopped

For decoration
3 ½ oz (100 g) Weiss Ceïba
42 % milk chocolate
Gold dusting powder (gold glitter dust)
Sosa® caramelized pecan nuts, cut into small shards
Edible gold leaf

Preparing and baking the banana bread

Soak the golden raisins in water for 1 hour. Drain, pat them dry with paper towel, then chop into small pieces. Preheat the oven to 325 °F (165 °C/ Gas Mark 3).

Peel and, using a fork, mash the bananas with the lemon juice. Sift the flour, baking powder, and baking soda together. Melt the butter to 104 °F (40 °C), then add the oil. Beat the eggs and sugar together using an electric beater until they are smooth and light.

Combine all the ingredients (flour mixture, mashed bananas, chopped golden raisins, almond powder, cinnamon, mascarpone, butter and oil, beaten eggs, and chocolate chips), gently mixing them together. Pour the batter into the cake pans and bake in the oven for 40 minutes. Unmold and let cool on a wire rack.

Preparing the chocolate ganache with cinnamon milk

Soak the gelatin in cold water for 10 minutes.

Bring the ⅔ cup (160 ml) cream to a simmer, add the squeezed-out gelatin, the cinnamon, and milk chocolate. Mix with a hand-held blender. Whisk in the 1 ¼ cups (290 ml) cream with the pecan praline until you have a homogenous mixture. Combine this mixture with the previous one and blend them together using a hand-held blender. Let the ganache firm up at room temperature for 24 hours before using.

Preparing the dark chocolate ganache

Bring the cream to a boil with the vanilla paste, glucose syrup, and trimoline. Using a hand-held blender, mix in the butter and chocolate. Let the ganache rest for 12 hours at room temperature before using.

Preparing the milk chocolate coating

Melt the chocolate to 104 °F (40 °C). Add the remaining ingredients and mix everything together. The coating needs to be used at 95 °F (35 °C).

Assembling and finishing

Melt the milk chocolate and coat the cakes.

To make the decoration, temper the Ceïba chocolate and spread it in a thin layer over an acetate sheet. Cut out stars of different sizes, some with open centers, and partly dust them with gold powder (gold glitter dust). Leave to set.

Spread a thick, domed layer of cinnamon milk ganache over the cakes and leave to set. Transfer the chocolate ganache to the pastry bag fitted with the ribbon tip and pipe the ganache in waves over the cakes. Finish decorating with the stars, shards of caramelized pecan nuts, and a few small pieces of edible gold leaf.

Recipe photographs, following pages.

Kevin Lacote

Pastry chef and proprietor of KL Pâtisserie, Paris

Because I like working with tangy chocolates that have a strong taste and plenty of character, dark Galaxie is one of my favorites. It fits these sablés like a glove.

Chocolate praline
SABLÉS

SERVES 6

Preparation time : 1 hour
Resting time : 24 hours
Cooking time : 20 minutes

Hazelnut praline
1 cup (7 oz/200 g) hazelnuts
¾ cup (5 oz/140 g) sugar
2 ¼ tablespoons (35 ml) water
Pinch (1 g) fleur de sel
Pure vanilla extract (enough
to stop the caramel cooking)

Chocolate praline
3 oz (80 g) Weiss Galaxie
41 % milk chocolate
7 oz (200 g) hazelnut praline
(see recipe above)

Chocolate sablé crumble
1 cup (4 ¼ oz/120 g) all-purpose
flour (T55)
3 ½ tablespoons (24 g)
Weiss cocoa powder
Scant 1 ½ cups (4 ¼ oz/120 g)
hazelnut powder
Pinch (1 g) fleur de sel
4 ¼ oz (120 g) softened butter
¾ cup (4 oz/110 g) brown sugar

Dark chocolate decoration
7 oz (200 g) Weiss Galaxie
67 % dark chocolate

Preparing the hazelnut praline
(make the day before)

Roast the hazelnuts on a baking sheet in a 325 °F (170 °C/Gas Mark 3) oven for 10 minutes. Cook the sugar with the water to a 338 °F (170 °C) caramel, using an instant-read thermometer to check the temperature. Add the hazelnuts, fleur de sel, and finally the vanilla extract. Remove from the heat, transfer to a baking sheet, and let cool, then grind in a food processor to obtain a homogenous praline. Use at a temperature of 92 °F (33.5 °C).

Preparing the chocolate praline
(make the day before)

Melt the chocolate to 92 °F (33.5 °C) and, making sure the hazelnut praline is at the same temperature, mix the two together. Keep for 24 hours at room temperature.

Preparing the chocolate sablé crumble
(start the day before)

Sift the flour, cocoa powder, hazelnut powder, and the fleur de sel together.

In a stand mixer fitted with the paddle beater, beat the butter and brown sugar together until the mixture is pale and light. Add the sifted ingredients. When the mixture is evenly combined, roll it out between two sheets of parchment paper ⅛ in (3 mm) thick and let rest in the refrigerator for 24 hours. Cut out 12 disks, 3 in (8 cm) in diameter, using a fluted cookie cutter, place on a Silpain® silicone baking mat and bake in a 325 °F (170 °C/Gas Mark 3) oven for 10 minutes.

Preparing the dark chocolate decoration
(make the day before)

Temper the chocolate and spread it with a rolling pin between two acetate sheets. Let the chocolate set, then cut out 12 disks, 2 ½ in (6 cm) in diameter, using a fluted cookie cutter. Let set for 24 hours.

Assembling

Pipe the chocolate praline over a chocolate sablé and cover the praline with another sablé. Stick the chocolate decorations on top with a little praline.

Marion Goettlé

Chef and proprietor of the Café Mirabelle, Paris

The indulgence and spiciness of Adzopé dark chocolate seemed to me the perfect choice for the brownie, the taste of which had to harmonize with the ganache flower. For that, I chose Madalait milk chocolate for its rounded, sweet flavor and beautifully creamy texture.

BROWNIE FLOWERS

with caramel sauce

SERVES 6

Preparation time :
1 hour 20 minutes
Chilling time : 24 hours
Cooking time : 30 minutes

8 × 12-in (20 × 30-cm) rimmed
baking sheet

Whipped milk chocolate ganache
1 sheet (2 g) leaf gelatin
Scant ½ cup (100 ml) whipping
cream + 1 ¼ cups (300ml)
to add at the end
6 oz (170 g) Weiss Madalait
35 % milk chocolate, chopped
Fleur de sel to taste

Chocolate brownies
⅔ cup (3 oz/82.5 g)
all-purpose flour
½ teaspoon (1.5 g) fine salt
½ teaspoon (2 g) baking powder
4 ½ oz (125 g) pecan nuts
3 ¾ oz (105 g) butter
4 ½ oz (125 g) Weiss Adzopé
55 % dark chocolate
2 ¾ oz (75 g) whole egg
(about 1 ½ eggs)
Scant 1 cup (6 oz/165 g)
superfine sugar

Caramel
⅔ cup (4 ½ oz/125 g)
superfine sugar
⅓ cup (75 ml) whipping cream
2 oz (60 g) slightly salted butter

Preparing the whipped milk chocolate ganache
(make the day before)

Soak the gelatin in cold water for 10 minutes. Bring the scant ½ cup (100 ml) whipping cream to a boil, add the squeezed-out gelatin, then pour this mixture over the chocolate and fleur de sel in three equal quantities, mixing to make a smooth ganache. Add the remaining cream and mix using a hand-held blender. Press a sheet of plastic wrap over the surface of the ganache and chill for 24 hours.

Preparing the chocolate brownies

Sift the flour with the salt and baking powder. Roast the pecans in a 325 °F (160 °C/Gas Mark 3) oven for 10 minutes, then chop them. Melt the butter and chocolate together in a bain-marie. Whisk the eggs with the sugar until they are pale and thicken, then add the sifted flour. Finally add the pecan nuts. Pour the mixture into the 8 × 12-in (20 × 30-cm) rimmed baking sheet and bake in a 340 °F (170 °C/Gas Mark 3) oven for 20 minutes. Let cool, then cut out 6 disks, 6 cm in diameter, using a cookie cutter. Set aside.

Preparing the caramel

Cook the sugar without any water until it is a brown caramel. Meanwhile, heat the cream to avoid a thermal shock when it is added to the caramel. When the sugar is well caramelized, take it off the heat, add the butter and mix with a whisk, then add the hot cream. Let cool completely in the refrigerator.

Assembling and finishing

Whisk the ganache, then transfer it to a pastry bag fitted with a flat tip. Pipe "petals" on each brownie disk in the shape of a flower. Place the caramel in another pastry bag and pipe a little in the center of each flower.

Patrice Cabannes

Executive pastry chef at the Atlantis Hotel in Dubai, UAE

Cashew praline, which is fruity and has a good nutty taste, seemed the obvious choice to me for monkey bread. Mahoë chocolate, despite its strong cocoa aroma, still retains its milky flavor so it adds a creamy note, and its toasted aftertaste makes the praline stand out.

CHOCOLATE *with cashew praline* MONKEY BREAD

SERVES 4

Preparation time : 2 hours
Resting time : 12 hours +
1 hour 30 minutes
Cooking time : 30 minutes
Freezing time : at least 4 hours

Pavoni® silicone Bamboo log mold
PX4318

Chocolate spread
⅓ cup (2 oz/57.5 g) superfine sugar
3 tablespoons (42 ml) water
Scant 1 ¾ cups (437.5 ml)
whipping cream
1 ½ oz (37.5 g) glucose syrup
6 ¾ oz (187.5 g) Weiss Mahoë
43 % milk chocolate
1 lb ½ oz (465 g) Weiss gianduja
6 tablespoons + 1 teaspoon
(95 ml) vegetable oil

Whipped milk chocolate ganache
2 cups (500 ml) whipping cream
3 ½ oz (100 g) trimoline
1 lb 6 oz (625 g) Weiss Mahoë
43 % milk chocolate, chopped
4 cups (1 liter) whipping cream,
well chilled (to whip)

Chocolate pan de sal dough
4 cups (1 lb 2 oz/500 g)
all-purpose flour (T55)
⅓ cup (1 ⅓ oz/37.5 g) Weiss
cocoa powder
⅓ cup (2 ¾ oz/75 g)
superfine sugar
⅓ oz (10 g) fresh yeast
½ cup (2 oz/60 g) powdered milk
1 ⅔ teaspoons (7.5 g) S 500
(bread improver)
Generous 1 cup (275 ml)
warm water

Chocolate rock frosting
9 oz (250 g) Weiss Li Chu
64 % dark chocolate
1 ¾ oz (50 g) Weiss cocoa butter
¾ cup (2 oz/60 g) chopped almonds
1 teaspoon (5 ml) vegetable oil

For baking the monkey breads
Muscovado sugar
Chopped cashews
Melted butter

For finishing
Weiss cashew praline with fleur
de sel de Guérande
Cashew nuts
Gold dusting powder
Chocolate decorations

Preparing the chocolate spread
(make the day before)

Mix the sugar and water in a saucepan and bring to a boil to make a syrup. Let cool. Bring the cream and glucose syrup to a boil and pour over the syrup and the rest of the ingredients in a mixing bowl. Blend until smooth using a hand-held blender, cover with plastic wrap, and keep overnight in the refrigerator.

Preparing the whipped milk chocolate ganache
(make the day before)

In a saucepan, bring the first quantity of cream and trimoline to a boil. Pour over the chocolate and mix until smooth. Add the chilled cream and stir until it is fully incorporated. Let rest overnight in the refrigerator. The next day, whip the ganache in a stand mixer until it is firm.

Preparing the chocolate pan de sal dough

In a stand mixer, beat all the ingredients together for 4 minutes at low speed and then for 12 minutes at medium speed. Cover the dough and let rise for at least 45 minutes, until it has doubled in volume.

Preparing the chocolate rock frosting

Melt the chocolate, then add the oil and almonds.

Baking the monkey breads

Shape the pan de sal dough into a long sausage, ½ in (1 cm) in diameter and cut into small pieces, ½ in (2.5 cm) long.

Fill 4 cavities of the Pavoni silicone Bamboo log mold with a bed of muscovado sugar and chopped cashews (to make long thin shapes).

Dip the pieces of dough in the melted butter and line them up in the mold on the muscovado sugar and cashew nut beds. Fill the mold in this way, making sure that the surface of the dough is level. (If you have any dough left over, make a bed of muscovado sugar and chopped cashews in another cavity to make 5 monkey breads.) Dust with muscovado sugar and cashews.

Place in a steam oven heated to 35 °F (95 °C), then bake for 30 minutes in a standard oven at 340 °F (170 °C/ Gas Mark 3), placing a wire rack on top of the mold to keep the surface level. Unmold and immediately place in a deep freezer or freezer.

Assembling and finishing

Make 4 cylinders (or 5, depending on the number of monkey breads) from an acetate sheet, ¾ in (1.5 cm) in diameter and the same length as the molds, and fill with chocolate spread. Place in the freezer.

When the monkey breads are frozen, remove them from the mold, and pipe a line of whipped ganache down the length of each. Remove the cylinders of chocolate spread from the acetate tubes and place in the center of the ganache, pressing down to fix the chocolate spread firmly in place. Mask the monkey breads with ganache on each side, smoothing it neatly so that each one looks like a single piece.

Keep the monkey breads in the freezer. Melt the chocolate rock frosting until it is liquid but still only just warm.

Using a toothpick, turn the monkey breads over, dip them in the frosting, and place them on a serving plate. They must look like long thin cakes coated with chocolate. Decorate the top of each with cashew praline with fleur de sel de Guérande, cashew nuts dusted with gold powder, and chocolate decorations. Let set.

Recipe photographs, following pages.

Clément Le Déoré

Pastry chef and proprietor of Desserts By Clément in San Diego, United States

Suprême milk chocolate is ideal for a milk chocolate mousse as the texture of the chocolate makes the mousse beautifully creamy.

THE FINEST

MAKES 1 CAKE

Preparation time : 2 hours
Chilling time : 12 hours
Cooking time : 30 minutes
Freezing time : 4 hours

Flexipan® mold measuring
10 × 14 in (25 × 35 cm)
Silikomart® silicone mold Universo
1200, 7 in (18 cm) in diameter
Baking ring, 6 in (15 cm)
in diameter

Milk chocolate frosting
3 sheets (5.9 g) leaf gelatin
3 ½ tablespoons (50 ml) water
½ cup (3 ½ oz/100 g) sugar
3 ½ oz (100 g) glucose syrup
2 ½ oz (67 g) sweetened
condensed milk
3 ½ oz (100 g) Weiss Suprême
38 % milk chocolate, chopped

Chocolate sponge cake
5 tablespoons (1 ½ oz/40 g)
all-purpose flour
3 ¾ tablespoons (1 ½ oz/40 g
potato starch
3 tablespoons (20 g) Weiss
cocoa powder
3 oz (93 g) egg white
(about 3 whites)
6 ½ tablespoons
(2 ¾ oz/77 g) sugar
2 oz (64 g) egg yolk
(about 3 yolks)

Milk chocolate mousse
4 tablespoons (60 ml)
whipping cream
2 ¾ cup (650 ml) whole milk
Scant 1 oz (24 g) egg yolk
(about 1 ¼ yolks)
2 ½ teaspoons (10 g) sugar
9 oz (250 g) Weiss Suprême
38 % milk chocolate, chopped
Generous ¾ cup (200 ml)
whipped cream

Ganache
4 tablespoons (60 ml)
whipping cream
4 tablespoons (60 ml) whole milk
4 ½ oz (130 g) Weiss Acarigua 70 %
dark chocolate, chopped

For assembling and finishing
4 ½ oz (127 g) Weiss cashew praline
with fleur de sel
Weiss Galaxie 67 % dark chocolate
for decoration
Gold dusting powder

Preparing the milk chocolate frosting
(make the day before)

Soak the gelatin in a bowl of very cold water.

In a saucepan, bring the water, sugar, and glucose syrup to a boil and cook to 235 °F (113 °C). Pour over the condensed milk, squeezed-out gelatin, and chocolate. Mix everything together with a hand-held blender and refrigerate the frosting overnight. It must be used at between 86 and 95 °F (30 and 35 °C).

Preparing the chocolate sponge cake

Sift the flour with the potato starch and cocoa powder. Whisk the egg whites with the sugar to firm peaks in a stand mixer. Add the egg yolks and continue whisking at medium speed for 20 seconds. With the mixer switched off, fold in the dry ingredients using a spatula. Pour the batter into the 10 × 14 in (25 × 35 cm) Flexipan and bake in a 325 °F (170 °C/Gas Mark 3) oven for 25–30 minutes. Let cool, then cut a disk, 6 in (15 cm) in diameter, using the baking ring. Leave the disk of sponge in the ring.

Preparing the milk chocolate mousse

Bring the cream and milk to a boil in a saucepan. Whisk the egg yolks with the sugar until they whiten. Gradually pour the cream and the milk over the yolks, whisking constantly. Return the mixture to the saucepan and cook to 180 °F (82 °C), as for making a crème anglaise. Pour the mixture over the chopped chocolate, mixing until evenly combined. Let the mousse cool to 95 °F (35 °C), then fold in the whipped cream and keep chilled.

Preparing the ganache

Bring the cream and milk to a boil in a saucepan. Pour over the chocolate, mixing thoroughly with a hand-held blender. Pour 9 oz (250 g) of the ganache over the sponge in the baking ring. Place in the freezer.

Assembling and finishing

Spread the cashew praline with fleur de sel into the baking ring on top of the frozen ganache. Return it to the freezer until the whole is frozen hard. Unmold immediately before assembling.

Pour 7 oz (200 g) milk chocolate mousse into the 7-in (18-cm) silicone mold and place the insert (the sponge, ganache, and praline) in the mousse. Smooth to the edges and freeze for at least 4 hours. The assembled cake must be completely frozen before it is frosted.

Cover the cake with the frosting and leave until set. Make a band from tempered Galaxie dark chocolate, 8 in (20 cm) long and 1 ¼ in (3 cm) wide, and fit it around the base of the cake. Also make chocolate decorations using Galaxie dark chocolate inspired by those in the photograph. Dip the tips of them in gold dusting powder and stick them onto the cake. Finish by decorating the whole (making a ring around the top of the cake and dusting the chocolate band) with gold dusting powder.

Recipe photograph, page 109.

Patrice Cabannes

Executive pastry chef at the Atlantis Hotel in Dubai, UAE

Anëo white chocolate is extraordinary for its creaminess and, for a white chocolate, it is not very sweet, which allows it to combine well with honey. In addition to the aroma, its color is also important in producing the clean white finish of the gateaux.

HONEY WHITE CHOCOLATE, *coconut, and yuzu gateaux*

SERVES 6

Preparation time : 2 hours
Cooking time : 1 hour 40 minutes
Resting time : 12 hours
Freezing time : at least 4 hours

6 Pavoni® silicone KE032 Galaxy molds (measuring 7 × 2 ¾ in/ 17.4 × 6.85 cm)
Pavoni® Gourmand GG047 Honeycomb mold

Whipped white chocolate ganache
2 ½ sheets (5 g) leaf gelatin
1 cup (250 ml) whipping cream
2 ½ oz (65.5 g) glucose syrup
6 ½ oz (175 g) Weiss Anëo 34 % white chocolate, chopped
2 cups (500 ml) whipping cream, well chilled

Coconut dacquoise
1 ½ cups (4 ¾ oz/135 g) powdered almonds
Scant 1 cup (4 ¾ oz/135 g) coconut powder
2 cups (9 ½ oz/270 g) confectioners' sugar
½ cup (2 oz/60 g) all-purpose flour (T55)
10 ½ oz (300 g) egg white (about 10 whites)
½ cup (3 ¾ oz/105 g) superfine sugar

Coconut and almond praline crisp
1 ½ oz (45 g) Weiss Anëo 34 % white chocolate
1 ¾ oz (50 g) caramelized puffed rice
3 ½ oz (90 g) feuilletine
6 ½ oz (180 g) Weiss Valencia 50/50 crunchy almond praline
3 ½ tablespoons (50 ml) coconut oil
Scant ⅓ cup (1 ½ oz/40 g) coconut powder, roasted
Pinch (1 g) salt

White chocolate mousse
3 ¼ sheets (6.5 g) leaf gelatin
1 cup (250 ml) whole milk
325 g Weiss Anëo 34 % white chocolate, chopped
Generous 1 ½ cups (375 ml) whipped cream

Yuzu crémeux
1 ½ sheets (3 g) leaf gelatin
9 oz (250 g) yuzu purée
13 oz (375 g) whole egg (about 7 ½ eggs)
¾ cup (5 ¼ oz/150 g) sugar
5 ¼ oz (150 g) butter

Preparing the whipped white chocolate ganache
(start the day before)

Soak the gelatin in very cold water for at least 10 minutes. In a saucepan, bring the first quantity of cream and the glucose syrup to a boil. Pour them over the white chocolate and mix carefully. Add the chilled cream and fold it in until completely combined. Let rest overnight in the refrigerator. The next day, whip the ganache in a stand mixer until it is firm but not excessively so.

Preparing the coconut dacquoise

Sift together the powdered almonds, coconut powder, confectioners' sugar, and flour. In a stand mixer, whisk the egg whites with the sugar to make a meringue. Gently fold in the dry ingredients, using a flexible spatula. Transfer the mixture to a rimmed baking sheet lined with parchment paper (about 2 ¼ lb/1 kg of mixture), spread the surface level, and bake in a 400 °F (200 °C/Gas Mark 6) oven for 8 minutes.

Preparing the coconut and almond praline crisp

Melt the white chocolate, add the puffed rice, and the feuilletine, then the praline, coconut oil, roasted coconut powder, and salt. Spread the mixture over the dacquoise in an even layer.

Preparing the white chocolate mousse

Soak the gelatin in very cold water for at least 10 minutes. Bring the milk to a boil, pour it over the chocolate, and mix, adding the squeezed-out gelatin. When the ingredients are evenly combined, set aside until lukewarm. When it is still just warm, incorporate the whipped cream using a flexible spatula.

Preparing the yuzu crémeux

Soak the gelatin in very cold water for at least 10 minutes. Heat the yuzu purée. In a mixing bowl, whisk the eggs and sugar until pale and thick. When the purée starts to boil, lower the heat and, whisking constantly, incorporate the beaten egg mixture to make a creamy mixture. Add the squeezed-out gelatin and mix until dissolved. Take off the heat and mix in the butter, cut into small pieces. Blend everything together using a hand-held blender, cover with plastic wrap, and keep in the refrigerator. Make 6 cylinders from an acetate sheet, each ¾ in (2 cm) in diameter, and fill them with the crémeux. Freeze, remove the cylinders, and briefly let them thaw. When they are sufficiently soft, curve them into a perfect circle so they can be inserted into the mold. Freeze again.

Recipe photograph, page 113.

Continuation of the recipe
HONEY WHITE CHOCOLATE, COCONUT, AND YUZU GATEAUX

Honey mousse

8 ¾ sheets (17.5 g) leaf gelatin
3 ½ oz (100 g) honey
2 oz (62.5 g) egg yolk
(about 3 yolks)
Generous 1 ½ cups (375 ml)
whipped cream

White chocolate spray

9 oz (250 g) Weiss Anëo
34 % white chocolate
9 oz (250 g) Weiss cocoa butter

Honey and caramel tuiles

¼ cup (1 ¾ oz/50 g) superfine sugar
1 oz (25 g) melted butter
1 oz (25 g) all-purpose flour (T55)
1 ½ oz (40 g) honey

For finishing

Fresh coconut shavings

Preparing the honey mousse

Soak the gelatin in very cold water for at least 10 minutes. Heat the honey and whisk it in a stand mixer at maximum speed, adding the egg yolks to obtain a sabayon. Add the squeezed-out gelatin and warm gently, then carefully fold in the whipped cream.

Preparing the white chocolate spray

Melt the two ingredients together. The mixture needs to be used warm.

Preparing the honey and caramel tuiles

Whisk together the sugar and melted butter. Add the flour, then the honey, and mix carefully. Keep the mixture in the refrigerator for 1 hour. Spread it over the honeycomb mold and bake in a 210 °F (100 °C/Gas Mark ¼) oven for 90 minutes.

Assembling and finishing

Cut the crisp-covered dacquoise to the size of the molds, two pieces for each. Pipe the honey mousse into the base of each mold, then add a piece of dacquoise. Pipe the white chocolate mousse over the dacquoise, then add the frozen yuzu crémeux. Cover with white chocolate mousse, followed by the second piece of dacquoise. Press down lightly to eliminate any air bubbles and make the dacquoise adhere well. Freeze. When the gateaux are frozen solid, unmold them and dip each one, rounded side down, in the warm whipped ganache until half-coated. The surface should look slightly wavy, with peaks. Freeze. When the ganache is very firm, spray all over with white chocolate to give an attractive velvety appearance. Decorate each with fresh coconut shavings and a honey and caramel tuile.

Hari Unterrainer

Executive pastry chef of the Crown Resorts Chain in Melbourne, Australia

The Sacher sponge benefits from the power of Bassam chocolate with its balance of sweetness and bitterness, while the roundness and power of Ébène dark chocolate stand out in the frosting. The two blend attractively in this great classic.

Vegan
SACHER-TORTE

MAKES ONE 8-IN (20-CM) ROUND CAKE

Preparation time : 40 minutes
Cooking time : 1 hour

8- in (20-cm) round cake pan

Sacher sponge
2 ½ cups (11 ¼ oz/320 g) all-purpose flour
2 ¾ teaspoons (10 g) baking powder
2 ⅓ oz (10 g) baking soda
6 ½ oz (180 g) Weiss Bassam 69 % dark chocolate
6 ½ oz (180 g) vegan or vegetable margarine
1 ¼ cups (300 ml) almond milk
⅔ cup (4 ½ oz/120 g) sugar
6 ½ oz (180 g) apple compote
4 teaspoons (20 ml) natural vanilla extract
8 oz (220 g) apricot jam (with at least 50 % fruit)

Chocolate frosting
4 tablespoons (60 ml) water
Scant 1 cup (6 oz/160 g) sugar
2 ½ oz (65 g) glucose syrup
5 oz (150 g) Weiss Ébène 72 % dark chocolate

For serving
Vegan whipped cream

Preparing the Sacher sponge

Sift the flour with the baking powder and baking soda into a mixing bowl. Melt the Bassam dark chocolate with the vegan butter or vegetable margarine in the microwave.

Whisk the almond milk, sugar, apple compote, and vanilla extract into the melted chocolate, mixing well.

Preheat the oven to 340 °C (175 °C/ Gas Mark 3). Grease the round cake pan with vegan butter or vegetable margarine and line the base and sides with parchment paper. Place the cake pan on a baking sheet. Pour the Sacher mixture into it and bake in the oven for 55–60 minutes. Check the baking by pushing the blade of a knife into the center, which will come out clean if the sponge is done.

Remove from the oven, turn upside down onto a wire rack without unmolding the sponge, and leave to cool completely.

Run the blade of a knife between the cake pan and the parchment paper, unmold the cake and remove the paper. Cut the sponge in half horizontally. Place the top half next to the bottom half and spread the bottom half with some of the apricot jam. Replace the top half to reshape the cake.

Bring the rest of the apricot jam to a boil and brush it all over the Sacher sponge.

Preparing the chocolate frosting

Bring the water, sugar, and glucose syrup to a boil in a saucepan. Remove from the heat, add the chocolate, and mix with a whisk. When the mixture is homogenous, pour it onto a marble slab and temper the chocolate by stirring with a metal spatula. The icing will become shinier. Pour the warm frosting over the Sacher sponge, spread it quickly with two or three strokes of a palette knife, then frost around the edges. Place the sponge on a cake stand or serving plate and leave until the frosting is completely set.

The cake should be served at room temperature, accompanied with plenty of whipped (vegan) cream!

Marie Dieudonné

Pastry chef and proprietor of Sucré Cœur, Paris

In this cake, chocolate is king and its most important ingredient, adding several different textures and flavors. It therefore must be powerful, cocoa-rich, long in the mouth, and oaky, with a touch of bitterness, which is why I have chosen the two Weiss Galaxie chocolates, dark and milk.

GASPARD

SERVES 6

Preparation time :
1 hour 30 minutes
Resting time : 12 hours
Freezing time : 4 hours
Cooking time : 26 minutes

6 cylindrical silicone molds,
2 ½ in (6 cm) in diameter
6 cylindrical silicone molds,
2 ¾ in (7 cm) in diameter

Chocolate whipped cream
Scant ½ cup (100 ml)
whipping cream
3 oz (75 g) Weiss Altara
63 % dark chocolate
Generous ¾ cup (200 ml)
whipping cream, well chilled

Pâte sucrée
1 tablespoon + 2 teaspoons
(25 ml) vegetable oil
2 tablespoons (1 oz/30 g)
superfine sugar
4 ¾ tablespoons (70 ml) water
1 oz (25 g) butter, well chilled
and diced
1 oz (30 g) chestnut flour
1 cup (5 ¼ oz/150 g) corn flour
½ cup (1 ¾ oz/50 g)
powdered almonds
¾ teaspoon (4 g) salt

Chocolate sponge
4 ½ oz (130 g) butter
4 ½ oz (130 g) Weiss Galaxie
67 % dark chocolate, chopped
4 ½ oz (130 g) whole egg
(about 2 eggs)
Scant ½ cup (3 oz/84 g)
superfine sugar
¼ cup (1 ½ oz/40 g) potato flour
⅔ oz (20 g) trimoline
½ teaspoon (2 g) salt

Crémeux
6 tablespoons (90 ml) milk
Generous ¾ cup (190 ml)
whipping cream
1 oz (25 g) egg yolk (about 1 ½ yolks)
1 tablespoon (12 g) superfine sugar
2 ¼ teaspoons (7 g) cornstarch
1 oz (25 g) Weiss Altara 63 %
dark chocolate
1 oz (25 g) butter, diced

Chocolate ganache
Scant ½ cup (100 ml)
whipping cream
¼ teaspoon (1.5 g) salt
3 ½ oz (85 g) Weiss Galaxie
67 % dark chocolate, chopped
1 ½ oz (43 g) Weiss Galaxie
41 % milk chocolate, chopped
⅔ oz (17 g) butter

Cocoa sauce
7 oz (200 g) glucose syrup
at 86 °F (30 °C)
Scant 1 cup (3 ½ oz/100 g)
Weiss cocoa powder

Coating
7 oz (200 g) Weiss Galaxie
67 % dark chocolate, chopped
3 ½ oz (100 g) Weiss cocoa butter

For finishing
Cocoa powder
Caramelized cocoa nibs
Cornflower petals

Preparing the chocolate whipped cream

(make the day before)

Bring the first quantity of cream to a boil and pour it over the chocolate. Mix carefully, then add the second quantity of cream. Mix and let rest overnight in the refrigerator.

Preparing the pâte sucrée

In a stand mixer fitted with the paddle beater, mix the oil, sugar, water, and chilled butter together. Mix the flours with the powdered almonds, add to the mixer and mix just long enough to make a smooth dough. Shape the dough into a ball, cover it in plastic wrap, and let rest for at least 1 hour in the refrigerator. Roll the dough between two sheets of baking parchment to a thickness of ⅛ in (3 mm).

Cut out 6 disks using a 3-in (8-cm) round cookie cutter and freeze them until firm.

Place the disks on a silicone baking mat or baking sheet lined with parchment paper and bake in a 325 °F (160 °C/Gas Mark 3) oven for about 15 minutes. Set aside.

Preparing the chocolate sponge

Melt the butter and chocolate together in a bain-marie. Whisk the eggs with the sugar until they are pale and mousse-like. Sift the flour with the trimoline and salt and fold into the whisked egg mixture. Spread over a baking sheet (measuring about 12 × 16 in/ 30 × 40 cm) lined with parchment paper and bake in a 340 °F (170 °C/Gas Mark 3) oven for 11 minutes. Let cool.

Preparing the crémeux

Bring the milk and cream to a boil. Whisk the egg yolks with the sugar and cornstarch until the mixture is pale and thick. Whisking constantly, add the hot milk and cream a little at a time, then cook until thickened. Let the temperature cool to 104 °F (40 °C). Melt the chocolate, then, using a hand-held blender, incorporate it into the crème pâtissière with the diced butter. Let cool.

Preparing the chocolate ganache

Bring the cream to a boil with the salt. Blending constantly using a hand-held blender, pour over the two chocolates and butter blending until you have a smooth ganache.

Preparing the cocoa sauce

Heat the syrup and cocoa powder, mixing well. Let cool, then transfer to a pastry bag.

Assembling and finishing

Using a cookie cutter, cut 6 disks of sponge, 2 ½ in (6 cm) in diameter, for the inserts. Pour the crémeux into the 6 cylindrical molds, 2 ½ in (6 cm) diameter, then close the molds with the sponge disks. Freeze. When frozen, unmold the inserts and pipe the ganache into the 6 cylindrical silicone molds, 2 ¾ in (7 cm) in diameter, to half-fill them. Place the inserts into the ganache, pressing down until the ganache rises to the height of the sponge, smooth, then freeze until solid.

Unmold and prick the frozen assembled cakes with a fork. Melt the coating ingredients together and pour over until the cakes are evenly covered.

Transfer the chocolate whipped cream to a pastry bag fitted with a ¾-in (18-mm) plain tip and decorate the cakes with piped cream. Dust with cocoa powder and add small piped dots of cocoa sauce. Decorate with caramelized cocoa nibs and cornflower petals.

Recipe photograph, page 119. **117**

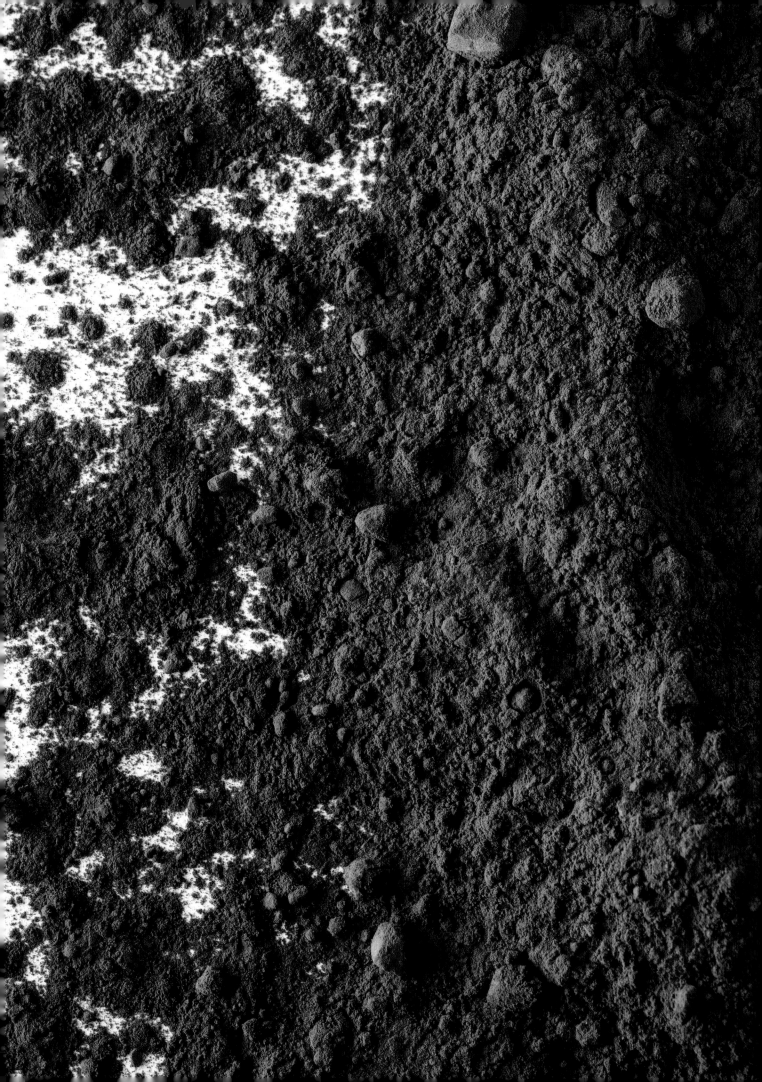

Loïc Beziat

Pastry chef and co-proprietor of the Beziat Frères Pâtisserie, Cahors

The characteristic smoky taste of Santarém chocolate seemed to me to be an essential ingredient when I was creating this reinterpretation of the classic Black Forest gâteau.

BLACK FOREST

SERVES 6

Preparation time : 2 hours
Resting time : 24 hours
Cooking time : 15 minutes

6 stainless steel baking rings, 2 ¾ in (7 cm) in diameter and 1 ¾ in (3.5 cm) deep

Chocolate sponge
2 ½ oz (63 g) Weiss Santarém 65 % dark chocolate
9 oz (252 g) egg white (about 8 ½ whites)
1 ⅓ cups (9 oz/252 g) superfine sugar
3 ½ oz (105 g) organic free-range whole egg (about 2 eggs)
7 oz (210 g) egg yolk (about 10 ½ yolks)
⅓ cup (1 ½ oz/42 g) traditional French flour
1 cup (3 oz/84 g) powdered almonds
⅓ cup (1 ½ oz/42 g) cocoa powder extra-rouge, sifted
¼ cup (63 ml) sunflower oil

Chocolate crémeux
Scant ½ teaspoon (2 g) powdered gelatin 200 Bloom
2 teaspoons (11 ml) water
Scant 1 cup (215 ml) reconstituted milk (1 ½ tablespoons/21.5 g powdered milk, 26 % fat, mixed with a generous ¾ cup/193 ml water)
Scant 1 cup (215 ml) whipping cream
3 ½ oz (86 g) egg yolk (about 4 ½ yolks)
3 ½ tablespoons (1 ½ oz/43 g) superfine sugar
6 ½ oz (178 g) Weiss Santarém 65 % dark chocolate, chopped

Chantilly cream with mascarpone
1 ½ oz (8 g) powdered gelatin 200 Bloom
Scant 3 tablespoons (41 ml) water
Scant 1 cup (225 ml) whipping cream
½ cup (3 ½ oz/100 g) superfine sugar
⅛ oz (4 g) Papua New Guinea vanilla bean
4 ¼ oz (125 g) mascarpone
2 ¼ cups (526 ml) whipping cream, well chilled

Chantilly cream with kirsch
2 cups (515 ml) Chantilly cream with mascarpone
2 ½ teaspoons (13 ml) kirsch
2 teaspoons (10 ml) semi-skimmed milk, well chilled

For finishing
200 g (7 oz) Griottines cherries in kirsch + a few extra for decoration
Weiss Santarém 65 % dark chocolate shavings
Edible gold leaf

Preparing the chocolate sponge

Melt the chocolate in a bain-marie. In the bowl of a stand mixer, whisk the egg whites to firm peaks with the sugar, then add the whole eggs and egg yolks. Next add the flour, powdered almonds, and sifted cocoa powder. Finally, mix in the melted chocolate and sunflower oil. Spread the batter over a baking sheet lined with parchment paper and bake in a 320 °F (160 °C/Gas Mark 3) oven for 15 minutes. Let cool. Cut out 12 disks of sponge (2 for each dessert) using a cookie cutter, 2 ¾ in (7 cm) in diameter.

Preparing the chocolate crémeux

Rehydrate the gelatin with the water. Bring the milk and cream to a boil. Whisk the egg yolks and sugar together in a mixing bowl until they whiten. Whisking constantly, add the hot liquid a little at a time. Cook, stirring constantly, until the mixture is thickened and smooth, as for making a crème anglaise. Pour this over the chopped chocolate and gelatin, blend with a hand-held blender, and keep chilled.

Preparing the Chantilly cream with mascarpone and kirsch

Rehydrate the gelatin with the water. Bring the scant 1 cup (225 ml) cream to a boil with the sugar and the vanilla bean, split lengthwise and seeds scraped out. Take off the heat, let infuse for 30 minutes, then strain. Add the rehydrated gelatin and the mascarpone, then blend with a hand-held blender. Add the 2 ¼ cups (526 ml) well-chilled cream, blend again, then let cool. Keep in the refrigerator for 24 hours. Before assembling the desserts, whip the 2 cups (515 ml) Chantilly cream with mascarpone with the kirsch, gradually adding the well-chilled milk. Use the Chantilly cream as soon as possible after preparing it.

Assembling and finishing

Place a disk of chocolate sponge in the bottom of each baking ring. Top each with 1 oz (30 g) chocolate crémeux, add ⅓ oz (10 g) Griottines, then cover with a second disk of sponge. Using a spoon, spread over the Chantilly cream, then freeze. Unmold and decorate each dessert with a chocolate shaving, a Griottine cherry, and a small piece of edible gold leaf.

Recipe photograph, following page.

Loïc Beziat

Pastry chef and co-proprietor of the Beziat Frères Pâtisserie, Cahors

This dessert needed to be made with sweet, creamy chocolates to balance the strong flavor of the coffee. I opted for two: Oryola white chocolate for its subtle nutty taste, which is in harmony with the hazelnut crisp, and Galaxie milk chocolate, as it is indulgent and not too sweet.

EXPRESSO

SERVES 6

Preparation time : 2 hours
Resting time : 40 minutes
Freezing time : 3 hours
Cooking time : 35 minutes

6 silicone half-spheres molds,
1 ¼ in (3 cm) in diameter
6 silicone half-spheres molds,
2 ¾ in (7 cm) in diameter

Hazelnut sponge

8 ½ oz (238 g) egg white (about 8 whites)
1 ¼ cups (8 ½ oz/238 g) superfine sugar
3 ½ oz (99 g) organic free-range whole egg (about 2 eggs)
7 oz (199 g) egg yolk (about 10 yolks)
⅔ cup (3 oz/79 g) traditional French flour
1 cup (2 ¾ oz/79 g) powdered hazelnuts
2 oz (60 g) butter, melted
3 oz (80 g) Weiss hazelnut paste

Hazelnut crisp

9 ½ oz (265 g) butter, softened
Generous 2 ¼ cups (9 ½ oz/265 g) traditional French flour
1 ¼ cups (6 ¼ oz/177 g) brown sugar
3 cups (9 ⅓ oz/265 g) powdered almonds
8 oz (228 g) Weiss Oryola 30 % white chocolate
6 ½ oz (184 g) Weiss hazelnut paste
1 ½ teaspoons (6 g) fleur de sel
9 ½ oz (266 g) raw hazelnuts, roasted and chopped

Coffee crémeux

1 teaspoon (5 g) powdered gelatin 200 Bloom
2 tablespoons (31 ml) water
6 ½ oz (179 g) Weiss Galaxie 41 % milk chocolate
1 ½ cups (357 ml) whipping cream
3 ½ oz (90 g) coffee beans
1 oz (27 g) coffee paste

Coffee mousse

Scant 2 ½ teaspoons (10.6 g) powdered gelatin 200 Bloom
3 tablespoons + 1 teaspoon (53 ml) water
1 lb 5 ½ oz (615 g) Weiss Galaxie 41 % milk chocolate
3 ¾ cups (916 ml) whipping cream, 35 % fat, whipped
1 ½ oz (45.6 g) powdered milk, 26 % fat
Scant 1 ¾ cups (410 ml) water
7 oz (196.2 g) coffee beans

Caramel glaze

Scant 1 teaspoon (4.4 g) powdered gelatin 200 Bloom
1 tablespoon + 2 teaspoons (26 ml) water
2 tablespoons (32 ml) water for the syrup
3 tablespoons (34.6 g) superfine sugar
1 ¼ oz (34.6 g) glucose syrup
1 ½ oz (42.2 g) sweetened condensed milk
Yellow and red liposoluble natural food colorings
2 ½ oz (64.6 g) Weiss Galaxie 41 % milk chocolate

For finishing

6 Weiss Galaxie 41 % milk chocolate rings, 2 ¾ in (7 cm) in diameter and 1 in (2.5 cm) wide
6 Weiss gianduja shavings

Preparing the hazelnut sponge

Whisk the egg whites with the sugar, add the whole eggs and egg yolks, then the flour, and finally the sifted powdered hazelnuts. Fold in the melted butter and hazelnut paste. Spread the batter over a baking sheet lined with baking parchment and bake in a 320 °F (160 °C/Gas Mark 3) oven for 15 minutes.

Preparing the hazelnut crisp

Rub the butter, flour, brown sugar, and powdered almonds together with your fingertips until the mixture has the texture of crumble. Spread it over a baking sheet and bake in a 320 °F (160 °C/Gas Mark 3) oven for 20 minutes. Meanwhile, melt the chocolate. Mix the hot crumble with the chocolate, hazelnut paste, *fleur de sel*, and chopped hazelnuts. Using a spatula, spread the mixture over the hazelnut sponge in a layer, 1/3 in (8 mm) thick. Keep chilled at 37.4 °F (3 °C).

Preparing the coffee crémeux

Rehydrate the gelatin with the water. Chop the chocolate and place in a bowl. Bring the cream to a boil with the coffee beans. Cover and let infuse for 20 minutes, then strain through a fine-mesh sieve. Pour over the chocolate, add the rehydrated gelatin, and the coffee paste. Blend using a hand-held blender and divide the mixture between the half-sphere molds, 1 ¼ in (3 cm) in diameter. Freeze.

Preparing the coffee mousse

Rehydrate the gelatin with the 2 ¼ cups (532 ml) water. Chop the chocolate and place in a bowl. Whip the cream. Mix the powdered milk and scant 1 ¾ cups (410 ml) water together to make a scant 2 cups (457 ml) of reconstituted milk. Bring this milk to a boil with the coffee beans, cover, and let infuse for 20 minutes, then strain through a fine-mesh sieve. Pour over the chocolate and add the rehydrated gelatin. Blend using a hand-held blender. When the temperature of the ganache drops to 90 °F (32 °C), fold in the whipped cream using a flexible spatula. Transfer to a pastry bag and keep chilled.

Preparing the caramel glaze

Rehydrate the gelatin with the 1 cup (258 ml) water. Bring the 1 ⅓ cups (324 ml) water, the sugar, and glucose syrup to a boil. Pour onto the rehydrated gelatin, add the condensed milk, food colorings, and chocolate. Blend using a hand-held blender and use this glaze at a temperature of between 95 and 104 °F (35 and 40 °C).

Assembling and finishing

Cut the sponge covered with hazelnut crisp into six 1 ⅓-in (3.5-cm) squares. Pipe 2 oz (60 g) coffee mousse into each of the 6 half-sphere molds, 2 ¾ in (7 cm) in diameter. Place a coffee crémeux insert in the middle of each, followed by a square of sponge covered with hazelnut crisp. Freeze, then coat with caramel glaze. Decorate each with a milk chocolate ring and a gianduja shaving.

Recipe photograph, page 123.

I like to make this recipe using Ibaria chocolate, which is very balanced so just right for this type of pâtisserie that contains praline. It has a slightly fruity flavor, which is exactly what is needed.

PAKÂNI

SERVES 6

Preparation time :
1 hour 30 minutes
Freezing time : 48 hours
Chilling time : 24 hours
Cooking time : 50 minutes

6 cylindrical molds, 2 in (5 cm)
in diameter
Tube, 3 in (8 cm) in diameter
6 cylindrical molds, 3 in (8 cm)
in diameter.

Pecan financier

1 ¾ oz (50 g) pecan nut halves
2 ¾ oz (75 g) butter
5 oz (141 g) egg white (about 4 ¾ whites)
Scant 1 cup (5 oz/138 g) brown sugar
Scant ½ cup (1 ¼ oz/36 g) pecan
nut powder
½ oz (15 g) almond powder
½ cup (2 oz/52 g) cake flour (T45)
⅓ oz (1.25 g) baking powder

Pecan praline

3 ½ oz (100 g) pecan nut halves
⅓ cup (2 ½ oz/70 g) sugar
1 tablespoon (17 ml) water
Pinch (0.5 g) salt
Pure vanilla extract (enough
to stop the caramel cooking)

Chocolate crumble

Scant ½ cup (2 oz/60 g) all-purpose
flour (T55)
1 ¾ tablespoons (12 g) Weiss
unsweetened cocoa powder
¾ cup (2 oz/60 g) hazelnut powder
Pinch (0.5 g) fleur de sel
2 oz (60 g) softened butter
⅓ cup (2 oz/55 g) brown sugar

Dark chocolate bands

3 ½ oz (100 g) Weiss Galaxie
67 % dark chocolate

Preparing the pecan financier
(make the day before)

Coarsely grind the pecan nuts in the bowl of a food processor. Preheat the oven to 325 °F (170 °C/Gas Mark 3).

Melt the butter and continue to cook it until it is nutbrown in color. Pour it into a shallow dish to cool quickly.

Lightly whisk the egg whites until they are foamy. In a stand mixer fitted with the paddle beater, mix the brown sugar, pecan nut powder, almond powder, flour, and baking powder together. Add the cold browned butter and then, gradually, the beaten egg whites. Pour this mixture into an 8 × 12-in (20 × 30-cm) frame set on a baking sheet lined with parchment paper and, using an angled spatula, spread it in an even layer. Scatter the chopped pecans all over the surface and bake in the oven for 15 minutes. Let cool.

Preparing the pecan praline
(make the day before)

Roast the pecan nuts on a baking sheet for 10 minutes in a 325 °F (170 °C/Gas Mark 3) oven. Cook the sugar with the water to a 338 °F (170 °C) caramel, using an instant-read thermometer to check the temperature. Add the pecans, fleur de sel, and finally the vanilla extract. Remove from the heat, transfer to a baking sheet, and let cool, then grind in a food processor to obtain a homogenous praline.

Weigh out 1 oz (25 g) praline, place this amount in each of the 6 cylindrical molds, 2 in (5 cm in diameter), and freeze for 24 hours. Using a cookie cutter, cut out 6 disks from the pecan financier, 2 in (5 cm) in diameter, and place these in the molds over the praline layer. Return the molds to the freezer.

Preparing the chocolate crumble
(make the day before)

Sift the flour, cocoa powder, hazelnut powder, and fleur de sel together.

In a stand mixer fitted with the paddle beater, beat the butter and brown sugar until the mixture is pale-colored and light. Add the sifted ingredients. When the mixture is evenly combined, pass it through a colander, a perforated tray, or sieve with large holes, and freeze the crumble. Shape it into 6 rounds, 2 in (5 cm) in diameter, on a Silpain® silicone baking mat and bake in a 325 °F (170 °C/Gas Mark 3) oven for 10 minutes. Freeze again.

Preparing the dark chocolate bands
(make the day before)

Temper the dark Galaxie chocolate and spread it over an acetate sheet using a flat spatula. Let set and then, using a wheel pastry cutter, cut 6 bands, 1 in (2.8 cm) wide, and roll them around a tube, 2 ½ in (6 cm) in diameter. Let set for 24 hours.

Continuation of the recipe **PAKÂNI**

Chocolate nib sablé

3 ½ oz (105 g) cocoa nibs

⅓ cup (1 ½ oz/45 g) flour

1 teaspoon (2.5 g) Weiss cocoa powder

1 ½ oz (40 g) softened butter

1 ¾ tablespoons (½ oz/14 g) confectioners' sugar

1 ¾ tablespoons (9 g) almond powder

1 ¾ oz (50 g) fleur de sel

1 ¾ oz (50 g) whole egg (about 1 egg)

Ibaria chocolate mousse

2 ¾ oz (74 g) Weiss Ibaria 67 % dark chocolate

Scant 1 cup (225 ml) whipping cream, well chilled

2 ¾ teaspoons (11 g) superfine sugar

1 teaspoon (5 ml) water

1 oz (25 g) whole egg, beaten (about ½ egg)

1 oz (27 g) egg yolk (about 1½ yolks)

Chocolate frosting

Generous ¾ cup (186 ml) whipping cream

⅔ cup (4 oz/ 116 g) sugar

4 ¾ tablespoons (70 ml) water

½ oz (12 g) Weiss cocoa powder, sifted

3 ¼ oz (93 g) Weiss Galaxie 67 % dark chocolate, chopped

½ oz (12 g) Weiss pure cocoa paste

3 tablespoons (43 g) powdered gelatin

3 ½ oz (105 g) neutral glaze

Dark chocolate spray

3 ½ oz (90 g) Weiss cocoa butter

2 oz (60 g) Weiss Galaxie 67 % dark chocolate, chopped

Preparing the chocolate nib sablé
(make the day before)

Roast the cocoa nibs on a baking sheet in a 325 °F (170 °C/Gas Mark 3) oven for 10 minutes. Let cool, then grind to a coarse powder in a food processor. Sift the flour and cocoa powder together. In a stand mixer fitted with the paddle beater, mix the butter, confectioners' sugar, almond powder, and fleur de sel together until they have a sandy texture. Add the eggs, then the flour and cocoa mixture, and finally the ground cocoa nibs. Gather the mixture together to make a dough and shape into a ball, wrap it in plastic wrap, and keep in the refrigerator for 24 hours. Roll the dough out ⅛ in (3 mm) thick and cut out 6 disks, 2 ½ in (6 cm) in diameter. Bake the sablés on a Silpain silicone baking mat for 10 minutes in a 325 °F (170 °C/Gas Mark 3) oven.

Preparing the Ibaria chocolate mousse

Melt the Ibaria chocolate in a bain-marie to 113 °F (45 °C), using an instant-read thermometer to check the temperature. Meanwhile, whip the cream with an electric hand beater in a mixing bowl until it thickens. Prepare a syrup by cooking the sugar and the water to 250 °F (121 °C), using an instant-read thermometer to check the temperature. Using a stand mixer fitted with the whisk attachment, whisk together the egg and the egg yolks. When they are light and mousse-like, pour in the syrup in a thin, steady stream, whisking constantly. The syrup must be at the required temperature to obtain a sabayon. Switch off the mixer and, using a flexible spatula, fold one third of the chocolate into the sabayon in the mixer bowl, then the remaining chocolate, and finally the whipped cream. Use immediately.

Preparing the chocolate frosting

Bring the cream to a boil. Prepare a syrup by cooking the sugar and water to 250 °F (121 °C), using an instant-read thermometer to check the temperature. Add the boiled cream, bring to a boil, add the cocoa powder, and return to a boil. Pour this mixture onto the chocolate and cocoa paste in a bowl and blend using a hand-held blender. Add the powdered gelatin and the neutral glaze and blend again. Pass through a fine-mesh sieve into a bowl, press plastic wrap over the surface, and keep in the refrigerator. The frosting must be used at a temperature of between 90 and 95 °F (32 and 35 °C).

Preparing the dark chocolate spray

Melt the cocoa butter, pour it over the dark chocolate, and blend until smooth using a hand-held blender. The spray needs to be used warm.

Assembling and finishing

Divide the chocolate mousse between 6 cylindrical molds, 3 in (8 cm) in diameter. Place a frozen praline disk in the middle of each. Cover with mousse, then with a chocolate nib sablé. Freeze for 24 hours. When finishing, spray the frozen crumble with the dark chocolate spray. Let set. Remove the cakes from the molds. Glaze the frozen cakes with the chocolate frosting, place the chocolate crumble in the middle, and surround with a chocolate band.

Executive pastry chef of the Crown Resorts Chain in Melbourne, Australia

In this vegan chocolate bar, the tangy notes and the freshness of Li Chu chocolate harmonize with those of lemon myrtle, an Australian bush herb.

Lemon myrtle vegan

CHOCOLATE BAR

MAKES 5 BARS

Preparation time : 30 minutes
Resting time : 45 minutes
Setting time : at least 2 hours

5 chocolate bar molds

Scant 1 cup (230 ml) almond milk

⅓ oz (10 g) powdered lemon myrtle

6 ¾ oz (190 g) VAO chocolate drops, 42 %

4 teaspoons (20 ml) refined coconut oil

Green colored chocolate

White colored chocolate

14 oz (400 g) Weiss Li Chu 64 % dark chocolate

⅔ oz (20 g) Weiss cocoa butter

In a saucepan, bring the almond milk to a boil, then whisk in the powdered lemon myrtle. Cover the saucepan with plastic wrap and leave to infuse for at least 30 minutes, preferably 45 minutes, to extract the maximum flavor from this "queen of lemon-scented herbs". Strain through a very fine-mesh sieve and heat in the microwave to about 140 °F (60 °C).

Add the VAO chocolate drops and refined coconut oil to the hot infusion. Blend with a hand-held blender until emulsified to obtain a smooth, homogenous ganache. Cover and leave until warm, between 77 and 82 °F (25 and 28 °C).

Melt the colored chocolates in separate bowls. Marble them over the inside of the chocolate bar molds and let set. Meanwhile, temper the Li Chu chocolate with the melted cocoa butter and add a thin layer to the molds. Fill the molds with lemon myrtle ganache. Cover with plastic wrap and leave the tablets for several hours until set.

Cover with a layer of tempered Li Chu chocolate and leave to set completely before unmolding.

We love the originality of the work done by Régis Marcon and Weiss, and Chococèpes give us the opportunity to explore new areas. Ativao dark chocolate is well balanced and suitable both for working with your hands, as well as using as a coating without it overwhelming the flavor of the fillings inside.

BELVEDERE

MAKES ABOUT 25 CHOCOLATES

Preparation time : 1 hour
Resting time : 12 hours

14-in (36-cm) square baking frame

Fillings
Generous 1 cup (270 ml) orange juice
4 ½ oz (118 g) powdered glucose
1 lb 5 oz (606 g) Weiss Chococèpes 42 % milk chocolate with ceps
1 ½ oz (43 g) Weiss cocoa butter
6 ½ oz (181 g) butter with 82 % fat, diced
½ oz (12 g) Weiss cocoa butter at room temperature

For coating and decoration
Weiss Ativao 67 % dark chocolate
Weiss Anëo 34 % white chocolate
Natural orange food coloring

Preparing the fillings
(make the day before)

Heat the orange juice and glucose in a saucepan until the glucose has dissolved.

Melt the Chococèpes chocolate with the first quantity of cocoa butter in a mixing bowl over a bain-marie. Pour the warm orange juice over the melted chocolate, a little at a time, mixing constantly. Add the butter, mixing it in using a hand-held blender. Warm the second quantity of cocoa butter, without letting the temperature of it rise above 93 °F (34 °C), then mix it into the ganache. When the temperature drops to 91 °F (33 °C), pour the mixture into the frame and let set overnight at a temperature of between 59 and 63 °F (15 and 17 °C).

Coating and decorating

Using a template as a guide, cut the ganache into individual shapes for filling the chocolates.

Melt the Ativao chocolate in one bowl and the Anëo chocolate in a separate bowl. Mix enough orange food coloring into the Anëo chocolate to tint it the desired shade.

Ensure that the temperature of the fillings is tempered to 68–70 °F (20–21 °C). Coat them with the Ativao chocolate, then decorate by drawing a diagonal line on top with the colored Anëo chocolate. Let set.

Weiss Galaxie milk chocolate is delicious and well balanced, contains just the right amount of sugar, and is excellent for decorating. We've chosen Anëo and Oryola white chocolates for their slight sweetness and their pretty color.

ALEXANDRE LE GLAND

**MAKES ABOUT
25 CHOCOLATES**

Preparation time :
1 hour 30 minutes
Resting time : 12 hours

14-in (36-cm) square baking frame

Praline filling
7 oz (195 g) Weiss Galaxie
41 % milk chocolate
3 ½ oz (100 g) Weiss cocoa butter
1 lb 5 oz (600 g) Weiss smooth
hazelnut praline from Piedmont
¼ teaspoon (1.2 g) Guérande
fleur de sel
3 ½ oz (100 g) Piedmont hazelnuts,
chopped
⅓ oz (10 g) Weiss cocoa butter

For coating and decoration
Weiss Oryola 30 % white chocolate
Weiss Galaxie 41 % milk chocolate
Weiss Anëo 34 % white chocolate
and Ativao 67 % dark chocolate
for the eyes

Preparing the praline filling
(make the day before)

Melt the Galaxie chocolate and the first quantity of cocoa butter to 113 °F (45 °C). Add the praline, fleur de sel, and hazelnuts. Temper the second quantity of cocoa butter, without letting the temperature of it rise above 93 °F (34 °C), and add it to the previous mixture. Let the temperature fall to between 77 and 82 °F (25 and 28 °C), then pour the mixture into the frame. Let set overnight. When it is completely hard, cut out Alexandre Le Gland shapes using a suitable template.

Coating and decorating

Melt the Oryola chocolate and temper it. Spread it into the frame in a thin layer. Before it has completely set, cut out the same shapes as before.

Melt and temper the Galaxie chocolate and spread this into the frame in a thin layer. Before it has completely set, cut out shapes for the hat of Alexandre Le Gland, again using a template. Once the chocolate has completely set, brush the hat shapes with a small wire brush and affix them to the Oryola shapes with a dot of chocolate.

Make the eyes by piping with small paper cones – Anëo white chocolate and then Ativao dark chocolate for the pupils.

Coat the insides with Galaxie milk chocolate and affix the decorations after coating. Let set.

Grégory Doyen

Travelling pâtissier and consultant to GD Sweet Concept

Santarém is a unique chocolate. In these little cakes its smoky taste is in perfect harmony with the fruity acidity of the morello cherries.

BLACK FOREST CHRISTMAS TREES

**SERVES 6
(MAKES 12 SMALL
CHRISTMAS TREES)**

Preparation time : 1 hour
Chilling time : 12 hours
Cooking time : 15 minutes

Silikomart® Globe 26 mold
Silikomart® Medium
Baba SF020 mold
Silikomart® 8 Christmas
trees 11317 mold

Chocolate brownie
2 oz (55 g) Weiss pure cocoa paste
5 oz (140 g) softened butter
4 oz (115 g) whole egg
(about 2 eggs)
3 ½ oz (100 g) brown sugar
½ teaspoon (2 g) salt
2 ¾ oz (75 g) cake flour (T45)
3 ½ tablespoons (25 g) Weiss
cocoa powder

Morello cherry inserts
¾ sheet (1.4 g) leaf gelatin
4 ¼ oz (120 g) Boiron morello
cherry purée
4 ½ oz (120 g) frozen Boiron
morello cherries
1 ¾ oz (50 g) trimoline
½ oz (15 g) superfine sugar
1 ¼ teaspoons (5 g) slow-set pectin
1 teaspoon (3 g) citric acid solution

Dark chocolate frosting
7 oz (200 g) Weiss cocoa butter
7 oz (200 g) Weiss Santarém
65 % dark chocolate

Anëo whipped ganache
1 ¼ sheets (2.25 g) leaf gelatin
½ vanilla bean (about 2 g)
1 ⅔ cups (400 ml) whipping cream,
35 % fat
3 oz (80 g) Weiss Anëo
34 % white chocolate, chopped

Assembling and finishing
12 morello cherries in liqueur
Confectioners' sugar

Preparing the chocolate brownie

Preheat the oven to 300 °F (155 °C/ Gas Mark 2). Melt the cocoa paste to 95 °F (35 °C) and place it in the bowl of a stand mixer fitted with the paddle beater. Add the softened butter and mix. In another bowl, whisk the eggs with the sugar and salt until the mixture whitens. With the motor running, pour the egg mixture into the contents of the stand mixer bowl and slowly add the remaining ingredients. Transfer the mixture to 12 cavities in the globe mold and bake in the oven for 15 minutes.

Preparing the morello cherry inserts

Soak the gelatin in cold water. Mix the morello cherry purée, the frozen morello cherries, and the trimoline together and heat to 104 °F (40 °C), using an instant-read thermometer to check the temperature. Mix the sugar with the pectin, add them to the cherry mixture, and pour in a bowl. Add the squeezed-out gelatin and citric acid. Leave to cool. Pour this compote into 12 baba mold cavities, then freeze.

Preparing the dark chocolate frosting

Chop both ingredients and melt them together. This frosting must be used at a temperature of 100.4 °F (38 °C).

Preparing the Anëo whipped ganache

Soak the gelatin in cold water for 10 minutes. Slit the vanilla bean lengthways and scrape out the seeds. Heat the cream to 149 °F (65 °C) with the vanilla bean and seeds. Pass through a fine-mesh sieve, pour the cream over the chopped chocolate, and add the squeezed-out gelatin. Mix with a hand-held blender. Let cool, then keep in the refrigerator for 12 hours before whipping.

Assembling and finishing

Unmold the morello cherry inserts. Stick a morello cherry in liqueur on the top of each using a drop of morello cherry compote. Freeze until assembling.

Whip the ganache with an electric hand beater until it is light and mousse-like. Transfer it to a pastry bag and partly fill 12 cavities in the Christmas tree molds. Add a morello cherry insert in the center of each, with the morello cherry facing downwards, and finish filling the molds with ganache. Position a brownie at the base, then freeze.

When the Christmas trees are frozen solid, heat the dark chocolate frosting to 100.4 °F (38 °C), unmold the Christmas trees and coat them completely with the frosting. Let set. Finishing decorating the trees by dusting with confectioners' sugar.

Recipe photographs, following pages.

Clément Le Déoré

Pastry chef and proprietor of Desserts By Clément in San Diego, United States

I opted for Galaxie dark chocolate, as it is easy to work with and is equally good whether you are making ganaches and mousses or chocolate decorations. I use it every day and I am very happy with it.

CHOCONUT

SERVES 6

Preparation time : 2 hours
Resting time : 24 hours
Cooking time : 20 minutes
Freezing time : 8 hours

6 Silikomart® Truffles 20 molds
6 Silikomart® Truffles 70 molds
1 Flexipan® measuring
10 x 14 in (25 x 35 cm)

Chocolate pâte sucrée

⅓ cup (1 ½ oz/45 g)
confectioners' sugar
2 ½ tablespoons (17.5 g) Weiss
cocoa powder
Pinch (1 g) fine salt
2 tablespoons (15 g)
almond powder
Scant 1 cup (3 ¾ oz/105 g)
all-purpose flour
2 oz (60 g) softened butter
1 oz (25 g) whole egg (about ½ egg)

Chocolate frosting

2.8 sheets (scant 6 g) leaf gelatin
⅔ cup (4 ¼ oz/120 g) superfine sugar
1 ½ oz (40 g) glucose syrup
Scant 3 tablespoons (40 ml) water
4 ¾ tablespoons (70 ml)
whipping cream
3 tablespoons (21 g) Weiss
cocoa powder
⅓ oz (10 g) neutral glaze
2 teaspoons (10 ml) vegetable oil

Preparing the chocolate pâte sucrée
(make the day before)

In a stand mixer fitted with the paddle beater, mix all the dry ingredients with the softened butter, then gradually add the egg. Remove the dough from the bowl, flatten it, and wrap it in plastic wrap. Let rest for 24 hours in the refrigerator.

Roll the dough out to a thickness of ¼ in (4 mm), cut out 6 disks, 3 in (8 cm) in diameter, using a cookie cutter, and bake on a Silpain® silicone baking mat in a 320 °F (160 °C/Gas Mark 3) oven for 7–8 minutes.

Preparing the chocolate frosting
(make the day before)

Soak the gelatin in very cold water for at least 10 minutes.

In a saucepan, combine the sugar, glucose syrup, and water and cook to 235 °F (113 °C). In a bowl, combine the cream, cocoa powder, glaze, squeezed-out gelatin, and oil. Pour the syrup into the bowl, mixing with a hand-held blender. Keep the frosting chilled overnight and use it at between 86 and 104 °F (35 and 40 °C).

Continuation of the recipe **CHOCONUT**

Chocolate mousse

⅔ cup (155 ml) whipping cream
4 oz (116 g) Weiss Galaxie
67 % dark chocolate, chopped
¾ oz (23 g) egg yolk (about 1 yolk)
¼ cup (1⅔ oz/46 g) superfine sugar
2 teaspoons (10 ml) water
1 ¼ cups (300 ml) whipping cream,
well chilled

Brownie

6 ½ oz (185 g) Weiss Galaxie
67 % dark chocolate
6 oz (165 g) butter
4 oz (120 g) whole egg
(about 2 eggs)
1 cup (6 ½ oz/185 g) superfine sugar
½ teaspoon (2 g) fine salt
4 ¾ tablespoons (70 ml)
whipping cream
½ cup (2 ¾ oz/75 g)
gluten-free flour

Hazelnut rock frosting

5 oz (140 g) Weiss Suprême
38 % milk chocolate
3 tablespoons (50 ml) vegetable oil
1 ½ oz (40 g) hazelnuts, chopped

Praline insert

4 ¼ oz (120 g) Weiss
hazelnut praline

For finishing

6 whole hazelnuts
Gold dusting powder

Preparing the chocolate mousse

Bring the ⅔ cup (155 ml) whipping cream to a boil and pour it over the chocolate. Mix to make a smooth ganache.

Make a pâte à bombe by whisking the egg yolks in a stand mixer until they are pale and mousse-like. Cook the sugar and water to 248 °F (120 °C), using an instant-read thermometer to check the temperature. With the mixer at slow speed, pour the sugar syrup into the egg yolk in a thin stream and continue whisking at medium speed until the mixture is cold.

For the next step, the ganache must be at a minimum temperature of 104 °F (40 °C). Whip the 1 ¼ cups (300 ml) cream with an electric beater until it holds firm but not stiff peaks. Fold the pâte à bombe into the ganache, adding a little of the whipped cream, then fold in the remaining whipped cream until evenly combined. Keep chilled.

Preparing and baking the brownie

Melt the chocolate and butter together. Whisk the eggs with the sugar and salt until the mixture whitens, then add the chocolate. Add the cream, whisking constantly, then the flour in the same way. Spread the mixture into the 10 × 14-in (25 × 35-cm) Flexipan mold and bake in a 320 °F (160 °C/Gas Mark 3) oven for 12 minutes. Let cool.

Preparing the hazelnut rock frosting

Melt the chocolate with the oil and add the hazelnuts. This frosting must be used at between 86 and 95 °F (30 and 35 °C).

Preparing the praline insert

Pipe ⅔ oz (20 g) hazelnut praline into each Truffles 20 mold, then freeze.

Assembling and finishing

Cut 6 individual brownies using a 1 ½ in (4 cm) round cookie cutter.

Unmold the frozen praline inserts. Pipe 2 ¾ oz (75 g) chocolate mousse into each cavity of the Truffles 70 silicone mold and insert a frozen praline marble in the mousse. Cover with a brownie disk and freeze.

When the Choconuts are frozen solid, unmold them and coat with the chocolate frosting. Wait for 2 or 3 minutes, then, using a toothpick, dip each Choconut in the hazelnut rock frosting until the bottom halves are coated, and place on a disk of pâte sucrée.

Place the hazelnuts in a small plastic box, add the gold dusting powder, seal the box, and shake it. Place a gilded hazelnut on top of each Choconut.

The dark Ébène chocolate lends itself beautifully to making the elegant decorations for this cake, being both fruity and floral. The creamy Anëo white chocolate produces a mousse that is rich and light with the scents of rose and vanilla.

Lychee and rose

LAYER CAKES

SERVES 6

Preparation time : 2 hours
Cooking time : 15 minutes
Freezing time : 4 hours

6 silicone half-spheres molds,
2 ⅓ in (6 cm) in diameter
6 Silikomart® Parfum 110
SF185 molds, 3 in (7.5 cm)
in diameter, with fluted sides

Lemon genoise
¼ cup (1 ½ oz/45 g) superfine sugar
3 ½ oz (105 g) egg yolk
(about 5 yolks)
⅔ cup (2 ¼ oz/62.5 g)
cake flour (T45)
Pinch (0.5 g) salt
1 ½ tablespoons (9 g) Fruit'Zest
Capfruit® (frozen lemon zest)
or freshly grated lemon zest
Scant 1 teaspoon (3.5 g)
baking powder
¼ cup (55 ml) vegetable oil

Meringue
4 ½ oz (132.5 g) egg white
(about 4 ¼ whites)
¼ cup (1 ½ oz/45 g) superfine sugar
Pinch (0.5 g) salt

Lychee mixture
5 oz (140 g) lychee and rose purée
2 teaspoons (10 g) superfine sugar
1 ½ teaspoons (5 g) pectin NH
Scant 1 teaspoon (5 g) frozen
grated IQF lemon zest (Sicoly®)
Scant ½ teaspoon (2.5 g) frozen
grated IQF orange zest (Sicoly®)
1 ¾ oz (50 g) fresh lychees, peeled,
pitted, and chopped

Preparing the lemon genoise

Mix the sugar and egg yolks together. Add the flour, salt, lemon zest, and baking powder, and then the oil, beating until the mixture is smooth. Make a firm meringue by whisking the egg whites with the sugar and salt. Gently fold the meringue into the egg yolk mixture until evenly combined, spread over a small baking sheet (measuring about 8 ¼ × 10 ½ in/21 × 27 cm), lined with parchment paper, and bake in a 325 °F (165 °C/Gas Mark 3) oven for 15 minutes. Let cool.

Preparing the lychee mixture

Bring the lychee and rose purée to a boil with the sugar, pectin, and zests. Add the fresh lychees, take off the heat, and blend until smooth with a hand-held blender. Let cool. Spoon the mixture into the 2 ⅓-in (6-cm) silicone half-sphere molds and freeze.

Continuation of the recipe **LYCHEE AND ROSE LAYER CAKES**

Rose and vanilla mousse with white chocolate

2 ½ sheets (5 g) leaf gelatin (140 Bloom)

¾ oz (22.5 g) egg yolk (about 1 yolk)

1 teaspoon (5 g) superfine sugar

½ vanilla bean, split and seeds scraped out

⅔ cup (160 ml) whipping cream

3 tablespoons (45 ml) whole milk

Generous 1 tablespoon (17.5 g) powdered milk

3 ½ oz (100 g) Weiss Anëo 34 % white chocolate

1 teaspoon (4 g) Sosa® rose paste

Generous ¾ cup (187 ml) whipped cream

Dark chocolate crunch

3 ½ oz (100 g) Weiss Ébène 72 % dark chocolate

3 ½ oz (100 g) Weiss cocoa butter

1 ½ oz (40 g) cookie crumbs

1 ½ tablespoons Weiss cocoa nibs

For assembling and finishing

7 oz (200 g) Weiss Ébène 72 % dark chocolate

Edible gold food coloring

1 teaspoon (5 g) Velly Spray® red cocoa butter velvet spray

1 oz (25 g) Weiss cocoa butter

Preparing the rose and vanilla mousse with white chocolate

Soak the gelatin in very cold water.

Mix the egg yolks, sugar, and vanilla seeds together. Heat the cream with the milk and powdered milk, stir in the egg yolk mixture, and cook until the temperature reaches 185 °F (85 °C). Remove from the heat. Melt the white chocolate with the rose paste and mix them together using a hand-held blender, then incorporate the egg and milk mixture. Squeeze out the gelatin and stir in until dissolved and evenly combined. Let cool to 95 °F (35 °C), then fold in the whipped cream. Spoon the mousse into the Silikomart® Parfum molds, inserting an unmolded half-sphere of frozen lychee mixture. Smooth the mousse to the edges, add a 2 ½-in (6.5-cm) disk of lemon genoise sponge, and finish by again smoothing the mousse to the edges. Keep in the refrigerator.

Preparing the dark chocolate crunch

Melt the chocolate and the cocoa butter together and mix in the other ingredients.

Assembling and finishing

Temper the dark chocolate and create ornaments (dragon teapot handle, dragon teapot spout, lid with a button), using a pastry bag. Let set, then paint them with gold food coloring.

Melt the cocoa butter and mix it with the red velvet spray. Unmold the pink mousse domes and, using a chocolate spray gun, spray them all over.

Melt the dark chocolate crunch and dip the base of each dome in the chocolate to coat them by a third up the side. Let set.

Arrange the chocolate ornaments on the cakes and let set.

Baptiste Brichon

Pastry chef and proprietor of the BAPT Pâtisserie in Macao, China

I wanted to bring together three very unique chocolates to make the bear cub, so I chose the two Galaxies for their strong aroma of raw cocoa, and Oryola for its hazelnut flavor.

BROWN BEAR *cub*

SERVES 6

Preparation time :
1 hour 40 minutes
Cooking time : 15 minutes
Freezing time : 4 hours

20 Silikomart® Truffles molds,
2 ½ in (6.2 cm) in diameter
and 2 in (5.3 cm) deep

Galaxie crémeux
Scant 1 cup (220 ml) whipping
cream 35 % fat
Scant 1 cup (220 ml) whole milk
3 ½ oz (90 g) egg yolk
(about 4 ½ yolks)
4 ½ oz (125 g) Weiss Galaxie
41 % milk chocolate
3 ½ oz (100 g) Weiss Galaxie
67 % dark chocolate

Sacher sponge
7 oz (200 g) almond paste 70 %
3 oz (80 g) egg yolk (about 4 yolks)
3 oz (80 g) whole egg
(about 1 ½ eggs)
1 ½ oz (40 g) butter
1 ½ oz (40 g) Weiss 100 % pure
cocoa paste
Scant ½ cup (1 ½ oz/40 g)
cake flour (T 45)
3 tablespoons (20 g) Weiss
cocoa powder
3 ½ oz (100 g) egg white
(about 3 ½ whites)
¼ cup (1 ¾ oz/50 g) superfine sugar

Galaxie dark chocolate crisp
1 ½ oz (45 g) Weiss Galaxie
67 % dark chocolate
⅓ oz (10 g) butter
4 ¼ oz (120 g) Weiss almond-
hazelnut praline 50-50
2 ¾ oz (75 g) feuilletine

Oryola mousse
5 sheets (10 g) leaf gelatin
1 cup (250 ml) whole milk
10 ½ oz (300 g) Weiss Oryola
30 % white chocolate with hazelnut
2 cups (500 ml) whipping cream
35 % fat

Galaxie dark chocolate spray
4 ½ oz (125 g) Galaxie 67 % dark
chocolate
4 ½ oz (125 g) Weiss cocoa butter

For assembling and finishing
Weiss Galaxie 41 % white
chocolate drops
Weiss Oryola 30 % white chocolate
with hazelnut
Chocolate coffee beans

Preparing the Galaxie crémeux

Bring the cream and milk to the boil. Whisk the egg yolks and gradually add the cream and milk, whisking constantly. Cook to 185 °F (85 °C) as for making a crème anglaise. Melt the two chocolates and mix in the crème anglaise in several additions using a hand-held blender. Keep in the refrigerator.

Preparing the Sacher sponge

Soften the almond paste in the microwave. Using an electric hand beater, whisk the almond paste with the egg yolks and whole eggs until thick and increased in volume. Melt the butter and cocoa paste to 104 °F (40 °C). Sift the flour and cocoa powder together. Whisk the egg whites with the superfine sugar until stiff, mix one third into the butter and cocoa paste mixture, then lightly fold into the almond and egg mixture. Fold in the remaining whisked whites and the sifted dry ingredients. Spread the mixture into an 8 × 12-in (20 × 30-cm) frame set on a Silpat mat and bake in a 350 °F (180 °C/Gas Mark 4) oven for 15 minutes.

Preparing the Galaxie dark chocolate crisp

Melt the chocolate and butter together to 86 °F (30 °C). Add the praline and then the feuilletine. Spread the mixture into an 8 × 12-in (20 x 30-cm) baking frame set on a Silpat® mat. Keep it in the freezer.

Preparing the Oryola mousse

Soak the gelatin in very cold water for 10 minutes. Bring the milk to a boil, squeeze out the gelatin leaves and add to the hot milk. Melt the chocolate and, using a hand-held blender, add the milk and blend to an emulsion. Cool to between 86 and 90 °F (30 and 32 °C). Whip the cream until mousse-like and fold into the mixture. Keep in the refrigerator.

Preparing the Galaxie dark chocolate spray

Melt the chocolate and cocoa butter to 104 °F (40 °C), stirring until mixed together.

Assembling and finishing

Spread 1 ¾ oz (50 g) of crémeux over the crisp in its frame and cover with the sponge. Spread the remaining crémeux over the sponge, then freeze. Cut into 1 ⅓ in (3.5 cm) squares. Pour 2 oz (60 g) of mousse into each of the Truffle molds and insert a crémeux-topped sponge square (crémeux down). Smooth the mousse over the top to the brim, then freeze the cakes.

Cut the chocolate drops in half for the ears. For the muzzles, mark a chocolate drop with a heated knife and stick in place with a little mousse.

Make the glasses from tempered Oryola chocolate.

Using a chocolate spray gun, spray the bears with the Galaxie dark chocolate spray, stick on a chocolate coffee bean for the nose of each bear, and finish by adding the glasses.

Recipe photograph, following page.

Baptiste Brichon

Pastry chef and proprietor of the BAPT Pâtisserie in Macao, China

Li Chu chocolate, with its hints of dried fuits, goes well with the coconut. For me, Anëo is the best white chocolate as it is not too sweet and has a good milky flavor.

LUCKY CAT

SERVES 6

Preparation time :
1 hour 40 minutes
Cooking time : 24 minutes
Freezing time : 4 hours

8 × 12-in (20 x 30-cm) baking frame
6 Silikomart® Stone molds,
2 ½ in (6.5 cm) in diameter
and 1 ¼ in (3 cm) deep
6 Silikomart® Mini Truffles molds,
1 ¼ in (3.2 cm) in diameter
and 1 in (2.8 cm) deep

Li Chu crémeux with coconut
9 oz (250 g) coconut purée
3 ½ tablespoons (50 ml)
whole milk
3 ½ oz (90 g) egg yolk
(about 4 ½ yolks)
6 ½ oz (180 g) Weiss Li Chu
64 % dark chocolate

Chocolate and coconut sponge
2 oz (60 g) egg yolk (about 3 yolks)
3 ½ oz (100 g) egg white
(about 3 ½ whites)
½ cup (2 ¾ oz/75 g)
superfine sugar
2 tablespoons (25 g)
coconut powder
¼ cup (1 oz/30 g) Weiss
cocoa powder

Cocoa-gianduja crisp
2 oz (60 g) cold butter, diced
2 ¾ tablespoons (¾ oz/25 g)
brown sugar
½ oz (15 g) coconut powder
Scant ½ cup (1 ½ oz/40 g)
cake flour (T45)
1 ½ tablespoons (10 g) Weiss
cocoa powder
Small pinch (0.25 g) fine salt
2 oz (60 g) Weiss dark gianduja
1 ½ oz (40 g) feuilletine

Coconut mousse
3 ¾ sheets (7.5 g) leaf gelatin
9 oz (250 g) coconut purée
½ oz (15 g) egg white
(about ½ white)
⅓ oz (10 g) trimoline
½ oz (15 g) superfine sugar
¼ oz (7.5 g) glucose syrup
Scant 1 cup (225 ml) whipping
cream 35 % fat

Anëo white chocolate spray
4 ½ oz (125 g) Weiss Anëo
34 % white chocolate
4 ½ oz (125 g) Weiss cocoa butter

For assembling and finishing
Weiss Anëo 34 % white chocolate
Red chocolate
Black chocolate
Edible gold powder

Preparing the Li Chu crémeux with coconut

Bring the coconut purée and whole milk to a boil. Whisk the egg yolks, then gradually pour in the coconut purée and milk, whisking constantly. Cook to 185 °F (85 °C) as for making a crème anglaise. Melt the dark chocolate and mix in the coconut crème anglaise in several additions using a hand-held blender. Keep in the refrigerator.

Preparing the chocolate and coconut sponge

Whisk the egg yolks. In another bowl, whisk the egg whites with the superfine sugar until stiff peaks form. Mix one third into the whisked egg yolks, then lightly fold in the rest with the coconut powder and sifted cocoa powder. Spread the mixture into an 8 × 12-in (20 x 30-cm) frame set on a Silpat mat and bake in a 350 °F (180 °C/Gas Mark 4) oven for 10–12 minutes.

Preparing the cocoa-gianduja crisp

Beat the butter, brown sugar, coconut powder, flour, cocoa powder, and salt in a stand mixer fitted with the paddle beater until the ingredients have the texture of a crumble. Roll out the crumble on a baking sheet and bake it in a 350 °F (180 °C/Gas Mark 4) oven for 12 minutes. Melt the gianduja to 86 °C (30 °C), then mix it with the crumble and the feuilletine. Spread the mixture into an 8 × 12-in (20 x 30-cm) frame on a Silpat® mat and, using a round pastry cutter, cut out six 2-in (5-cm) disks. Keep the disks in the freezer.

Preparing the coconut mousse

Soak the gelatin in cold water until softened. Bring the coconut purée to a boil, then cool to between 86 and 90 °F (30 and 32 °C). Whisk the egg white, trimoline, sugar, and glucose syrup in a stand mixer to make a cold meringue. Using a spatula, fold the coconut and meringue together. Squeeze out the gelatin leaves, melt, and fold in, mixing well. Whip the cream until mousse-like and fold into the mixture.

Preparing the Anëo spray

Melt the white chocolate and cocoa butter to 104 °F (40 °C), stirring until combined.

Assembling and finishing

Spread the crémeux over the sponge in its frame, then freeze the frame. Using a round pastry cutter, cut out six 2-in (5-cm) disks. Fill the Mini Truffle molds with coconut mousse to make the cat's head.

Pour 40 g (1 ½ oz) of mousse into each of the Stone molds, insert a mousse-topped sponge disk (mousse down), add a crumble and feuilletine disk, and spread with mousse to the rim of the molds. Freeze.

To make the cat's paws, pour tempered melted white Anëo chocolate into the truffle mold to make half-spheres ½ in (1 cm) diameter and fill straws with the same chocolate to make ¾-in (2-cm) sticks. Using a little mousse, stick one half sphere on the cat's body and another half sphere at the end of a stick and then on the opposite side of the cat's body. Using a chocolate spray gun, spray the cake with the Anëo and cocoa butter mixture.

Temper the red chocolate, and make hearts for the ears, a round band, ¼ in (0.5 cm) wide, for the collars, and thin rolls for the mouths. Stick these onto the cat as shown in the photograph. Make the eyes and claws with black chocolate. Finally, fix a half-sphere of golden Anëo chocolate to the collar for the bell.

Recipe photograph, page 149.

In these tarts, the well-rounded flavor of Ceïba milk chocolate overpowers neither the freshness of the jelly, nor the fruitiness of the poached pear. It remains long in the mouth, with slightly roasted notes that balance this classic and delicate partnership.

Pear and
CHOCOLATE TARTS

SERVES 6

Preparation time :
1 hour 30 minutes
Freezing time : 4 hours
Cooking time : 25 minutes

8 × 12-in (20 × 30-cm)
baking frame
6 cylindrical silicone molds,
2 ½ in (6 cm) in diameter
6 cylindrical silicone molds,
2 ¾ in (7 cm) in diameter

Pâte sucrée

1 tablespoon + 2 teaspoons
(25 ml) vegetable oil
2 tablespoons (1 oz/30 g)
superfine sugar
4 ¾ tablespoons (70 ml) water
1 oz (25 g) butter, well chilled
and diced
1 oz (30 g) chestnut flour
1 cup (5 ¼ oz/150 g) corn flour
½ cup (1 ¾ oz/50 g)
powdered almonds
¾ teaspoon (4 g) salt

Soft gluten-free sponge

3 oz (80 g) egg yolk (about 4 yolks)
5 teaspoons (20 g) superfine sugar
3 oz (80 g) egg white
(about 3 whites)
¼ cup (1 ½ oz/40 g) superfine sugar
⅓ oz (10 g) butter
4 teaspoons (20 ml) milk
¼ cup (1 ½ oz/42 g) potato flour

Preparing the pâte sucrée

In a stand mixer fitted with the paddle beater, mix the oil, sugar, water, and chilled butter together. Mix the flours with the powdered almonds, add them, and mix just long enough to make a smooth dough. Shape the dough into a ball, cover it in plastic wrap, and let rest for at least 1 hour in the refrigerator.

Roll the dough between two sheets of baking parchment to a thickness of ⅛ in (3 mm). Cut out 6 disks using a 3-in (8-cm) round cookie cutter and freeze them until firm. Place the disks on a silicone baking mat or baking sheet lined with parchment paper and bake in a 325 °F (160 °C/Gas Mark 3) oven for about 15 minutes. Set aside.

Preparing the soft gluten-free sponge

Whisk the egg yolks with the 5 teaspoons (20 g) sugar until they increase in volume and hold their shape. Whisk the egg whites, adding the 1 ½ oz (40 g) superfine sugar in three equal amounts. Once the whites are firm, gently fold them into the whisked yolks using a flexible spatula. Melt the butter with the milk until just warm, fold it into the egg mixture, and then sift the potato flour directly over. Fold everything together gently with a flexible spatula. Pour the batter into the 8 × 12-in (20 × 30-cm) baking frame set on a baking sheet covered with parchment paper. Bake in a 400 °F (200 °C/Gas Mark 6) oven for 7 minutes, then cut out 6 sponge disks, 2 ½-in (6 cm) in diameter, using a plain round cookie cutter for the inserts. Set aside.

Continuation of the recipe **PEAR AND CHOCOLATE TARTS**

Milk chocolate ganache

6 tablespoons (90 ml)
whipping cream
½ teaspoon (1.5 g) salt
4 ½ oz (127.5 g) Weiss Ceïba
42 % milk chocolate, chopped
¾ oz (22.5 g) butter

Pear jelly

3 ¾ oz (110 g) pear purée
½ teaspoon (1.5 g) pectin
2 ¼ teaspoons (11 g) superfine sugar

Poached pears

2 cups (500 ml) water
1 ⅓ cups (9 oz/250 g)
superfine sugar
½ teaspoon (2 g) ground cardamom
3 ripe, but firm, pears

Coating

7 oz (200 g) Weiss Galaxie
67 % dark chocolate, chopped
3 ½ oz (100 g) Weiss cocoa butter
½ teaspoon (2 g)
yellow food coloring

For finishing
Caramelized cocoa nibs
Rose petals

Preparing the milk chocolate ganache

Bring the cream to a boil with the salt. Pour it over the chocolate and mix until you have a smooth ganache. Add the butter, mixing everything together using a hand-held blender.

Preparing the pear jelly

Bring the pear purée to a boil with the pectin and sugar. Let cool in the refrigerator.

Preparing the poached pears

Make a syrup by bringing the water, sugar, and cardamom to a boil. Cut the pears into thin slices and poach them for a few moments in the hot syrup. Drain the pear slices and cool them quickly.

Assembling and finishing

Pour pear jelly into the 6 cylindrical silicone molds, 2 ½ in (6 cm) in diameter, and place the sponge disks at the bottom. Freeze.

Pour the ganache into the 6 cylindrical silicone molds, 2 ¾ in (7 cm) in diameter. Unmold the frozen pear jelly inserts and place on the ganache so the jelly touches the ganache. Press down until the ganache rises to the height of the sponge. Freeze until solid.

Melt the coating ingredients together. Unmold, prick the frozen assembled cakes with a fork, and pour the coating over them until they are evenly covered. Arrange the pear slices on top and glaze with just-melted jelly. Decorate with a few pieces of caramelized cocoa nibs and rose petals.

Christophe Roure

Chef and proprietor of Le Neuvième Art restaurant, Lyon

I envisaged this tart as a feminine dessert, one that is like a jewel. For this reason I chose Ativao chocolate, which is sensual and floral.

CHOCOLATE TART
with a gold tuile

SERVES 6

Preparation time : 40 minutes
Cooking time : 20 minutes
Freezing time : 1 hour

6 silicone macaron molds,
4 in (10 cm) in diameter
Square openwork stencil with
2 ½ × 2 ½-in (6 × 6-cm) squares

Madeleines

Scant ⅔ cup (3 oz/80 g)
all-purpose flour
3 tablespoons (¾ oz/20 g)
Weiss cocoa powder
⅓ cup (2 ⅔ oz/75 g)
superfine sugar
1 tablespoon (5 g) almond powder
⅔ teaspoon (2.5 g) baking powder
1 oz (25 g) trimoline
2 eggs
5 ½ tablespoons (80 ml)
grape seed oil

Chocolate caramel

7 oz (200 g) fondant
3 ½ oz (100 g) glucose syrup
3 ½ oz (100 g) Isomalt
3 ½ oz (90 g) Weiss 100 %
pure cocoa paste

Ganache

1 cup (250 ml) double cream
9 oz (250 g) Weiss Ativao
67 % dark chocolate, chopped
Scant ½ cup (100 ml) milk
1 egg

For finishing

Edible gold powder
Timut pepper

Preparing the madeleines

In a mixing bowl, whisk together the flour, cocoa powder, sugar, almond powder, and baking powder. Add the trimoline and the eggs and whisk until smooth. Add the oil and mix in vigorously until combined. Spoon into a pastry bag.

Preheat the oven to 350 °F (180 °C/ Gas Mark 4). Grease the silicone macaron mold with oil. Pipe 1 oz (30 g) of the madeleine mixture into each cavity, then tap to distribute it evenly. Bake for 3 minutes in the oven. Loosen the madeleines from the mold without removing them and turn the mold over onto a sheet of baking parchment so that the surface of the madeleines remains completely flat. Let cool.

Preparing the chocolate caramel

Heat the fondant, glucose syrup, and Isomalt in a small saucepan to 329 °F (165 °C), using an instant-read thermometer to check the temperature. Add the cocoa paste, mix quickly with a spatula, then tip out of the pan onto a Silpat® mat. When cold, reduce the caramel to a fine powder in a coffee grinder.

Preparing the ganache

Bring the cream to a boil in a saucepan, then pour it onto the chocolate and mix with a hand-held blender. Mix in the milk and egg in the same way. Cool, then vacuum pack to remove the air bubbles.

Before cooking the ganache, reheat it to 122 °F (50 °C). Preheat the oven to 250 °F (120 °C/Gas Mark ½). Place 1 ¾ oz (50 g) ganache in each of 6 cavities in the silicone macaron mold. Switch the oven off, place the mold inside, and leave the ganache in the oven for 10 minutes. Cool, then freeze.

Preparing the golden tuiles

Place the openwork stencil with 2 ½ × 2 ½-in (6 × 6-cm) squares on a Silpat mat and sprinkle with the chocolate caramel powder. Place in a 350 °F (180 °C/Gas Mark 4) oven until the caramel melts. Cool slightly, then place the caramel squares in a tuile mold. Let cool completely, then brush all over with edible gold powder.

Assembling and finishing

Unmold the ganaches onto the madeleines and leave to stand at room temperature until they reach serving temperature. Before serving, dust lightly with timut pepper, place a tuile on top, and serve immediately.

François Gagnaire

Chef and proprietor of Anicia restaurant, Paris

In this soufflé tartlets recipe, which is a tribute to Michel Bras's classic molten chocolate pudding, Ceïba white chocolate enhances the flavor of the blueberries, while the power and character of Li Chu chocolate are complemented by a fruity finish that blends well with the acidity of the berries.

SERVES 6

Preparation time : 1 hour
Resting time : 2 hours 15 minutes
Freezing time : 12 hours
Cooking time : 32 minutes

6 tartlet rings, 3 in (8 cm)
in diameter
6 cylindrical molds, 1 ½ in (4 cm)
in diameter

Chocolate pâte sucrée tartlet cases

¼ cup (1 oz/30 g) Weiss
cocoa powder
1 ¾ cups (8 oz/220 g)
all-purpose flour
4 oz (112 g) butter at room
temperature
Pinch (1 g) salt
¾ cup (3 ½ oz/100 g)
confectioners' sugar
1 egg

Ceïba white chocolate crémeux

1 sheet (2 g) leaf gelatin
Scant ½ cup (117 ml) whipping
cream
3 ½ tablespoons (50 ml) milk
2 oz (65 g) egg yolk (about 3 yolks)
3 ½ oz (100 g) Weiss Ceïba
33 % white chocolate, chopped
Wild blueberries to taste

Chocolate soufflé mixture

7 oz (200 g) Weiss Li Chu
64 % dark chocolate, chopped
Generous ¾ cup (200 ml) milk
1 tablespoon (10 g) cornstarch
1 ½ oz (40 g) egg yolk
(about 2 yolks)
4 ½ oz (135 g) egg white
(about 4 ¼ whites)
¼ cup (2 oz/55 g) superfine sugar
6 Weiss Ceïba 33 % white
chocolate drops

DOUBLE CHOCOLATE
soufflé tartlets with wild blueberries

Preparing the tartlet cases
(make the day before)

Sift the cocoa and flour together. Whisk the butter to soften it. Add the salt and confectioners' sugar, then, on low speed, add the flour mixture, and finally the egg. Gather the ingredients together to make a dough, shape into a ball, and flatten. Cover with plastic wrap and chill in the refrigerator for 4 hours. Roll out the dough ⅛-in (3-mm) thick and line into 6 tartlet rings, 3 in (8 cm) in diameter. Chill for 15 minutes, then prick the dough bases with a fork and chill again for 2 hours.

Preheat the oven to 325 °F (160 °C/ Gas Mark 3), upper and lower heating elements alight, and bake the tartlet cases for 20 minutes. When they come out of the oven, remove the baking rings, and let the tartlet cases cool on a wire rack.

Preparing the Ceïba white chocolate crémeux
(make the day before)

Soak the gelatin in cold water. Mix the cream, milk, and egg yolks together in a saucepan. Heat to 180 °F (82 °C), using an instant-read thermometer to check the temperature, then pour the mixture over the white chocolate. Add the squeezed-out gelatin and blend with a hand-held blender until emulsified. Pour a ⅝-in (1.5-cm) layer of the crémeux into 6 cylindrical molds, 1 ½ in (4 cm) in diameter. Sprinkle with wild blueberries and freeze for 12 hours.

Preparing and cooking the soufflés

Preheat the oven to 375 ° F (190 °C/ Gas Mark 5). Melt the Li Chu dark chocolate in a bain-marie. Stir the milk and cornstarch together until boiling and thickened. Pour over the egg yolks, whisking constantly. Set aside.

Whisk the egg whites in two stages, adding the sugar when they are foamy and then continuing to whisk until the egg whites form firm peaks, the tips of which fold over when the whisk is lifted ('au bec d'oiseau', in French). Using a flexible spatula, mix one third of the egg whites into the chocolate mixture, then lightly fold in the remainder. Spoon the mixture into a pastry bag.

Fill the tartlet cases with the soufflé mixture and place a Ceïba white chocolate drop in the centre of the blueberries, pressing it down lightly. Cover with a dome of soufflé mixture and bake in the oven for 12 minutes. Serve immediately.

Johanna Roques

Pastry chef and proprietor of Jojo & Co, Paris

The woody and warm notes of Li Chu chocolate combine so well with the brown cardamom in the ganache for my Viennese tart. My idea was to bring together all the flavors of a hot chocolate.

VIENNESE TARTS

SERVES 4

Preparation time :
40 minutes (the day before),
1 hour 10 minutes (the next day)
Resting time : 14 hours
Freezing time : 2 hours
Cooking time : 37 minutes

4 tartlet pans, not fluted,
and with straight sides, 2 ½ in
(6 cm) in diameter
4 Silikomart® Globe molds,
1 ½-in (4-cm) x ¾-in (2-cm)

Chocolate shortcrust pastry
4 ½ oz (130 g) cold butter, diced
½ teaspoon (2 g) salt
1 ⅓ cups (6 oz/170 g)
confectioners' sugar
¼ cup (1 oz/25 g) powdered almonds
3 tablespoons (⅔ oz/20 g) Weiss
cocoa powder
1 ½ cups (7 oz/195 g)
all-purpose flour
1 ¾ oz (50 g) whole egg
(about 1 egg)
Chocolate egg wash (1 egg beaten
with 1 pinch of salt and a little
chocolate brown food coloring)

**Chocolate crémeux infused
with brown cardamom**
¾ cup (175 ml) milk
½ cup (125 ml) whipping cream
1–2 pods (1 g) brown cardamom
(or black cardamom)
5 oz (150 g) Weiss Li Chu
64 % dark chocolate
2 oz (60 g) egg yolk (about 3 yolks)
2 tablespoons (1 oz/25 g)
superfine sugar

**Reconstituted shortcrust pastry
with chocolate and cocoa nibs**
2 oz (63 g) softened butter
¼ cup (1 ½ oz/43 g)
muscovado sugar
¼ cup (1 ½ oz/43 g) superfine sugar
1 cup (3 ½ oz/93 g)
powdered almonds
¾ oz (22 g) Weiss cocoa nibs,
ground to a powder
½ cup (2 ½ oz/67 g)
all-purpose flour
½ teaspoon (2 g) fleur de sel
4 oz (113 g) Weiss Li Chu 64 %
dark chocolate
1 ¾ oz (48 g) Weiss cocoa nibs

Preparing the chocolate shortcrust pastry

The day before, beat together the cold butter, salt, confectioners' sugar, powdered almonds, cocoa powder, and flour in a stand mixer until you have an evenly textured sandy mixture. With the motor running, add the egg and mix to make a dough. Shape the dough into a ball, cover it with plastic wrap, and keep overnight in the refrigerator.

The next day, roll the dough to a thickness of ⅛ in (3 mm) and use it to line the non-fluted tartlet molds. Bake them for 16 minutes in a preheated 340 °F (170 °C/Gas Mark 3) oven. Meanwhile, make the chocolate egg wash. Take the tartlet cases out of the oven and brush the egg wash over them before returning them to the oven for 5–6 minutes to finish baking.

Preparing the chocolate crémeux infused with brown cardamom

The day before, bring the milk and cream to a boil with the crushed brown cardamom (so that its aroma can infuse the cream). Take off the heat, cover, and let infuse for 30 minutes. Keep chilled, covered, overnight.

The next day, prepare the crémeux. Melt the chocolate. Whisk the egg yolks and sugar together until the mixture whitens. Bring the infused cream to a boil, strain it, then pour over the whisked yolks and sugar. Cook as for a crème anglaise until it thickens (without letting the temperature rise above 174 °F/79 °C), pour it over the melted chocolate, and mix lightly with a hand-held blender until homogenized. Pour the hot crémeux directly into the tartlet cases, then place in the refrigerator.

Preparing the reconstituted shortcrust pastry with chocolate and cocoa nibs

Place the softened butter in the bowl of a stand mixer and add both sugars. Beat until the mixture is light and creamy, then add the powdered almonds, ground cocoa nibs, flour, and fleur de sel to make a dough. Roll the dough as thinly as possible between two sheets of parchment paper and bake it on a baking sheet in a preheated 350 °F (185 °C/Gas Mark 4) oven for 15 minutes. Let cool, then chop the pastry coarsely before grinding it to a powder. Melt the chocolate and add to the powdered pastry, then the cocoa nibs. Roll the mixture thinly between two sheets of parchment paper to a thickness of 1/16 in (1–2 mm), then freeze it until hard. Once the pastry is hard, cut out 4 disks using a 2 ½-in (6-cm) cookie cutter. These will be placed in the tartlet cases.

Recipe photograph, page 163.

Continuation of the recipe **VIENNESE TARTS**

Melting caramel with dark chocolate insert

3 ½ tablespoons (50 ml) whole milk + 2 tablespoons (30 ml) to add to the cream

1 ½ tablespoons (11 g) Weiss cocoa nibs

1 oz (30 g) Weiss Li Chu 64 % dark chocolate

5 ½ tablespoons (81 ml) whipping cream

½ oz (12 g) glucose syrup + 1 ¼ oz (34 g) for the caramel

Pinch (1 g) fleur de sel

2 tablespoons (1 oz/30 g) superfine sugar

¾ oz (22.5 g) unsalted butter

Chantilly cream

½ cup (125 ml) whipping cream, well chilled

2 teaspoons (10 g) mascarpone

1 teaspoon (2.5 g) confectioners' sugar

For decoration

Weiss cocoa powder

Preparing the melting caramel with dark chocolate insert

Bring the 3 ½ tablespoons (50 ml) milk to a boil with the cocoa nibs. Let infuse for 1 hour before making the caramel insert. Melt the chocolate.

Bring the whipping cream, 2 tablespoons (30 ml) milk, ½ oz (12 g) glucose syrup, and fleur de sel to a boil.

In a separate saucepan, cook the 1 ¼ oz (34 g) glucose syrup and superfine sugar to 350 °F (180 °C) until a deep amber-colored and fluid caramel. Take off the heat, deglaze the caramel with the cream mixture, bring to a boil, and continue cooking until the temperature reaches 225 °F (107 °C). Add the melted chocolate and emulsify using a hand-held blender. Add the butter and blend again. Strain the cocoa nib-infused milk through a fine-mesh sieve and add it as well. Blend thoroughly using a hand-held blender, then pour the chocolate caramel directly into 4 cavities in the Silikomart Globe mold. Freeze until completely hard.

Preparing the Chantilly cream

Whip the cream and mascarpone with the confectioners' sugar in the bowl of a stand mixer. The Chantilly cream must be firm but still soft. Transfer it to a pastry bag fitted with a fluted tip.

Assembling and finishing

Place a frozen caramel insert in the middle of each tartlet case. Pipe the Chantilly cream in a large swirl around the inserts. Dust lightly with cocoa powder.

Chef at the restaurants Le Suquet, Laguiole, and La Halle aux Grains, Paris

Weiss Santarém chocolate seduced me with its smoky and toasted notes that replicate the roasted cereals used to make the crust for the tart base. It also has a vegetal side that partners well with the teas we serve during our Tea Time gatherings.

A TART IN LOVE WITH A GRAND CRU CHOCOLATE

from Papua New Guinea and a praline of puffed cereals

SERVES 6

Preparation time :
1 hour 30 minutes
Cooking time : 10 minutes
Freezing time : 2 hours

Flexipan® entremets sheet,
14 × 22 in (35 × 55 cm)

Chocolate ganache

1 lb 2 oz (500 g) Weiss Santarém
65 % dark chocolate
4 ¼ oz (120 g) butter
Scant ½ cup (100 ml) whipping cream, 35 % fat
7 oz (200 g) egg yolk (about 10 yolks)
6 ½ oz (180 g) egg white (6 whites)
½ cup (3 ½ oz/100 g) superfine sugar
1 ¾ oz (50 g) cocoa nibs, ground and sifted

Granola crust

4 ½ oz (120 g) egg white (4 whites)
2 tablespoons (25 ml) grape seed oil
2 ½ oz (68 g) acacia honey
7 oz (200 g) chopped almonds
7 oz (200 g) chopped hazelnuts
1 ⅓ cups (3 ½ oz/105 g) rolled oats
1 ¼ cups (3 ½ oz/105 g) buckwheat flakes
½ cup (2 oz/60 g) pumpkin seeds, chopped
½ cup (2 oz/60 g) dehydrated kasha
Scant ⅓ cup (2 oz/60 g) flax seeds
Scant ½ cup (2 oz/60 g) poppy seeds
½ cup (2 oz/60 g)
sunflower seeds, chopped
½ cup (3 oz/85 g) muscovado sugar
½ teaspoon (2 g) fleur de sel

Preparing the chocolate ganache

Melt the chocolate and butter together in a bain-marie. Add the cream, then the egg yolks, and mix well. In a stand mixer, beat the egg whites and sugar to firm peaks and fold into the chocolate mixture using a spatula. Pour the ganache over the entremets sheet and spread until smooth: it must be at least ¼ in (5 mm) thick. Sprinkle with the ground cocoa nibs and fast freeze. Once the ganache is frozen, unmold it from the sheet, and cut into 6 strips measuring 3 ½ × 2 in (9 × 5 cm). Keep these in the freezer.

Preparing the granola crust

Mix the egg whites, oil, honey, and muscovado sugar together and pour over the nuts, oats, flakes, and seeds. Mix everything together and spread out in a ¼-in (5-mm) layer. Use a 3 ½ × 6-in (9 × 15-cm) stencil to cut out rectangles and bake them in a 300 °F (150 °C/Gas Mark 2) oven for 10 minutes.

Continuation of the recipe
A TART IN LOVE WITH A GRAND CRU CHOCOLATE

Puffed cereal praline

1 oz (25 g) kasha

1 oz (25 g) sunflower seeds

1 oz (25 g) pumpkin seeds

1 oz (25 g) white sesame seeds

⅓ cup (2 ¾ oz/75 g) superfine sugar

Grape seed oil

Fleur de sel

For finishing

3 tablespoons (20 g) Weiss cocoa powder

2 ½ tablespoons (20 g) confectioners' sugar

¾ oz (20 g) Weiss cocoa nibs, ground to a powder

1 oz (25 g) pumpkin seeds, chopped and sifted

1 oz (25 g) roasted millet seeds

Preparing the puffed cereal praline

Roast all the seeds. Cook the sugar to a caramel and pour it over the roasted seeds. Let cool, then grind in a food processor. Add grape seed oil and fleur de sel to your liking to make a paste.

Assembling and finishing

Mix the cocoa powder, confectioners' sugar, and ground cocoa nibs together. Arrange the granola crusts on individual rectangular serving plates and sit the ganache rectangles flush on top. Place a ruler two-thirds along the width of each tart and dust with the cocoa-confectioners' sugar-cocoa nibs mixture. Place under a salamander broiler for 1 ½ minutes until a light crust forms on top. Using a pipette, pipe a line of praline down the length of each tart, sprinkle the praline with the pumpkin and millet seeds, and serve immediately.

Jonathan Chauve

Pastry chef and Master Chocolatier at Weiss

This tart pays homage to Ébène 72 % dark chocolate, which in 1985 was the chocolate with the highest percentage of cocoa solids on the market. Both rounded and powerful, Ébène gives any recipe a harmonious and gourmet chocolate flavor.

ÉBÈNE TARTS

with coffee and hazelnuts "Eugène's Walk"

SERVES 4

Preparation time : 2 hours
Freezing time : 4 hours
Chilling time : 12 hours
Cooking time : 25 minutes

22 × 14-in (56 × 36-cm)
stainless steel baking frame
4 stainless steel baking rings,
6 ¼ in (16 cm) in diameter, one side
covered with plastic wrap to form
a tight seal

Whipped Ébène ganache

½ cup (130 ml) whipping cream,
35 % fat + generous ¾ cup (200 ml)
whipping cream, well chilled
¼ cup (60 ml) whole milk
½ oz (12 g) trimoline
½ oz (12 g) glucose syrup 40DE
3 ½ oz (95 g) Weiss Ébène
72 % dark chocolate, chopped

Eugène's sponge bread

Scant ½ cup (2 oz/55 g) flour
1 ¼ teaspoons (4.5 g) baking powder
3 ½ oz (108 g) egg yolk
(about 5 yolks)
1 oz (25 g) trimoline
6 oz (170 g) egg white
(about 5 whites)
⅔ cup (4 ½ oz/125 g)
superfine sugar
Pinch (1 g) fine salt
2 ½ oz (63 g) butter
7 oz (195 g) Weiss 60–40 hazelnut
praline from Piedmont IGP
3 ½ oz (95 g) Weiss 100 %
hazelnut paste
5 ¼ oz (150 g) blanched hazelnuts,
roasted and chopped
Vegetable oil for the baking frame

Caramelized coffee beans

3 oz (80 g) coffee beans
½ cup (3 ½ oz/90 g) superfine sugar
Scant ½ cup (100 ml) water

Crunchy hazelnut praline with coffee splinters

1 oz (25 g) chopped caramelized
coffee beans (keep what is left over
for the gourmet coating)
½ teaspoon (2 g) fleur de sel
10 ½ oz (300 g) Weiss crunchy
praline hazelnut romanes 50–50

Coffee-Ébène ganache

Scant ⅔ cup (140 ml) whipping
cream, 35 % fat
⅔ cup (140 ml) whole milk
1 ¾ oz (50 g) coffee syrup (from
the caramelized coffee beans)
1 oz (30 g) glucose syrup 40DE
1 oz (30 g) trimoline
8 oz (230 g) Weiss Ébène
72 % dark chocolate, chopped

Preparing the whipped Ébène ganache

Bring the ½ cup (130 ml) cream to a boil with the milk, trimoline, and glucose syrup. Pour this mixture over the chopped Ébène chocolate and blend until smooth using a hand-held blender. Add the generous ¾ cup (200 ml) well-chilled cream and blend again until smooth. Keep chilled (at 39 °F/4 °C) in a container, with a sheet of plastic wrap pressed over the surface of the ganache, for at least 12 hours.

Preparing Eugène's sponge bread

Sift the flour and baking powder together. Preheat the oven to 340 °F (170 °C/Gas Mark 3).

In the bowl of a stand mixer fitted with the whisk, beat the egg yolks with the trimoline to the ribbon stage. In a separate bowl, whisk the egg whites until firm, gradually whisking in the sugar and salt. Melt the butter to 113 °F (45 °C). Mix the hazelnut praline, hazelnut paste, and melted butter together in a bowl. Mix in the whisked egg yolks and then gently fold in the meringue using a flexible spatula. Finally fold in the flour and baking powder. Lightly oil the baking frame, place on a silicone baking mat, and spread the batter into it. Dust with the chopped hazelnuts and bake in the oven for 12–15 minutes. Let cool, then cut 4 disks, 6 ¼ in (16 cm) in diameter, using a cookie cutter.

Preparing the caramelized coffee beans

Roast the coffee beans on a baking sheet for 5 minutes in a 300 °F (150 °C/Gas Mark 2) oven on fan setting, then chop them. Bring the sugar and water to a boil, add the chopped coffee beans, cover, and let infuse for 30 minutes. Drain (reserving the syrup for the ganache). Spread the chopped coffee beans over a silicone baking mat and roast in a 300 °F (150 °C/Gas Mark 2) oven for 8–10 minutes. Let cool, then store the caramelized chopped beans in an airtight container.

Preparing the crunchy hazelnut praline with coffee splinters

In a blender, lightly grind the caramelized coffee beans with the fleur de sel. Mix with the praline and transfer to a pastry bag. Keep in the refrigerator.

Preparing the coffee-Ébène ganache

Bring the cream, milk, coffee syrup, glucose syrup, and trimoline to a boil, pour the mixture over the Ébène chocolate, and stir to mix. Blend with a hand-held blender until smooth, then divide the ganache between the 4 baking rings, with the sides sealed with plastic wrap facing downwards. Place a disk of Eugène's sponge bread on top, then freeze.

Recipe photograph, page 171.

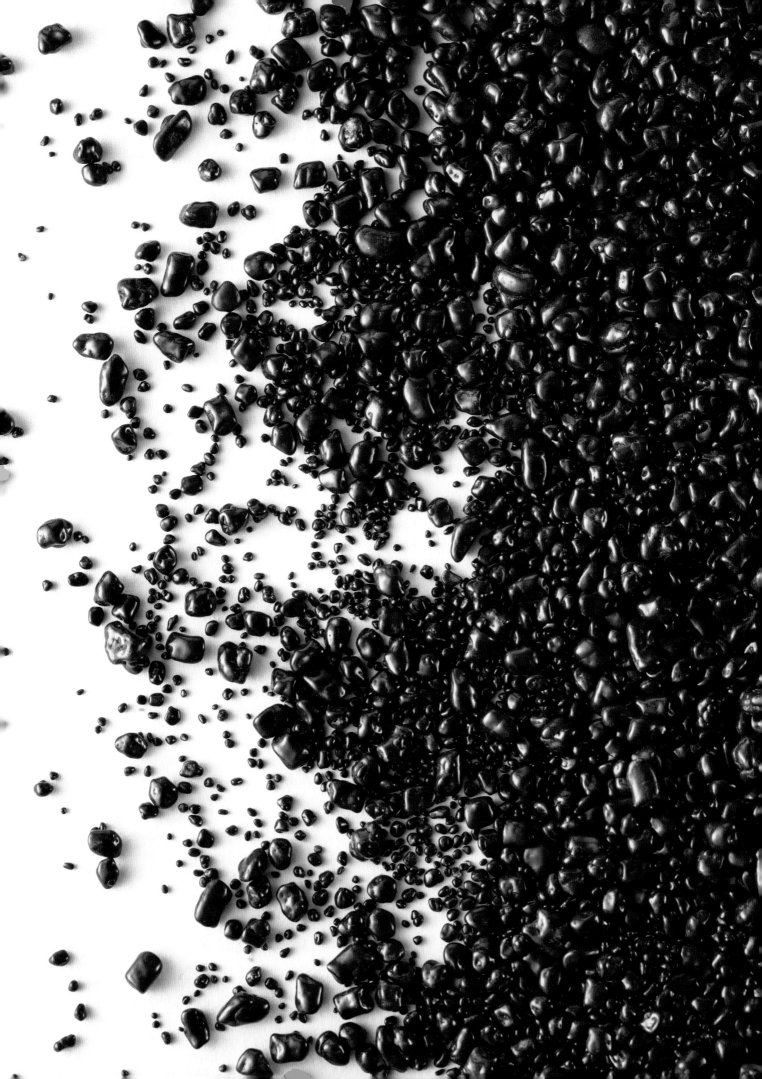

Continuation of the recipe **ÉBÈNE TARTS**

Gourmet coating

1 lb 2 oz (500 g) Weiss Ébène
72 % dark chocolate
5 ¼ oz (150 g) Weiss cocoa butter
3 tablespoons (50 ml)
grape seed oil
1 ¾ oz (50 g) hazelnuts,
chopped and roasted
1 ¾ oz (50 g) chopped caramelized
coffee beans (see step 3 of
the recipe)

Ébène chocolate curls

1 lb 2 oz (500 g) Weiss Ébène
72 % dark chocolate

Ébène chocolate spray

12 oz (350 g) Weiss Ébène
72 % dark chocolate
5 ¼ oz (150 g) Weiss cocoa butter

Chocolate mirror frosting

1 ¾ teaspoons (8 g) powdered
gelatin 200B
3 tablespoons (48 ml) cold water
½ cup (3 ½ oz/100 g)
superfine sugar
1 oz (30 g) glucose syrup DE40
½ cup (130 ml) whipping cream,
35 % fat
Generous ¾ cup (200 ml) water
Generous ½ cup (2 ½ oz/70 g)
Weiss cocoa powder

For finishing
Hazelnut "envelopes" (skins from
blanching whole hazelnuts)

Preparing the gourmet coating

Melt the chocolate and cocoa butter with the oil to 104–113 °F (40–45 °C). Add the hazelnuts and chopped caramelized coffee beans. Pour the mixture into a container large enough for dipping the frozen layered ganache and sponges.

Preparing the Ébène chocolate curls

Place 4 baking sheets in an oven preheated to 122 °F (50 °C/Gas on lowest setting). While they are heating, melt the Ébène chocolate in a bain-marie to 122 °F (50 °C).

Using an angled spatula, spread about 4 ¼ oz (120 g) of chocolate over each baking sheet in an even layer. Run a chocolate comb over two of the baking sheets to create ridges in the chocolate. Place all the chocolate-covered baking sheets in the refrigerator (at 39 °F/4 °C) for 20 minutes. Take them out of the refrigerator and let the chocolate return to room temperature (72–73 °F/22–23 °C), which will take about 20 minutes. Using a triangular scraper, shave off chocolate curls. Keep at 59 °F (15 °C) until assembling.

Preparing the Ébène chocolate spray

Melt the Ébène chocolate and cocoa butter together to 113 °F (45 °C). Transfer to a chocolate spray gun and spray the frozen desserts.

Preparing the chocolate mirror frosting

Soak the gelatin in the 3 tablespoons (48 ml) cold water to rehydrate it. Prepare a syrup by cooking the sugar, glucose syrup, and cream together with the generous ¾ cup (200 ml) water. When the mixture boils, add the cocoa powder and cook over high heat for 1 minute, stirring constantly. Strain and add the soaked gelatin. Blend with a hand-held blender and transfer to a chocolate spray gun. The mixture needs to be used at 104 °F (40 °C).

Assembling and finishing

Dip each frozen layered ganache and sponge in the melted gourmet coating to its full height. Let set.

Whisk the whipped Ébène ganache, without letting it stiffen too much. Transfer it to a pastry bag fitted with a ½-in (14-mm) plain tip and immediately pipe ropes on the dipped entremets, leaving about a ½-in (1-cm) space between each rope. Fill the gaps with hazelnut praline with caramelized coffee splinters. Arrange the chocolate curls attractively on top, then fast freeze.

Once frozen, spray the entremets with the chocolate mirror frosting, then decorate with a few hazelnut "envelopes".

Artisan baker at Le Pain d'Exclamation and President of the Jury of the Coupe de France des Écoles

Although Weiss' Shiny Cocoa Granules were designed for making hot chocolate, I like using them in Viennese pastries and plain sponge cakes. Due to their melting point and their ability to keep their shape in the oven (up to a temperature of 350 F/180 C/Gas Mark 4), the granules have great potential for artisan bakers and, as a result, I have been able to demonstrate the flexibility of Weiss' products.

VIENNESE *with shiny granules*
PETITS PAINS

SERVES 6

Preparation time : 40 minutes
Kneading time : 25 minutes
Rising and resting time :
2 hours 35 minutes
Cooking time : 16 minutes

2 cups (9 oz/250 g)
all-purpose flour
2 ¾ cups (9 oz/250 g)
cake flour (T45)
1 ⅓ cups (9 oz/250 g)
superfine sugar
2 teaspoons (10 g) fine salt
⅔ oz (20 g) fresh yeast
1 ½ teaspoons (10 g) Diamalt
or honey
Scant 1 cup (220 ml) low-fat milk
⅓ oz (10 g) free-range whole egg
(about ⅓ egg)
3 ½ oz (100 g) fermented dough
2 ½ oz (65 g) softened butter
4 teaspoons (20 ml) low-fat milk
for bassinage
7 oz (200 g) Weiss Shiny Cocoa
Granules, stored in the freezer
(so they do not stain the dough)
1 beaten egg for egg wash
Very fine wheat semolina

Place the flours, sugar, salt, yeast, Diamalt or honey, scant 1 cup (220 ml) milk, egg, and fermented dough in the bowl of a stand mixer fitted with the dough hook and begin kneading on speed 1 for 8 minutes. Continue kneading on speed 2 for an additional 8 minutes until the dough comes away from the sides of the bowl. Add the softened butter and continue kneading until the dough is very smooth and leaves the sides of the bowl completely. Depending on the texture and moisture content, add the milk for bassinage, or not, as needed. Quickly incorporate the frozen cocoa granules and immediately stop mixing. Transfer the dough to a mixing bowl, cover with plastic wrap, and chill in the refrigerator for 20 minutes.

Divide the dough into 3 ½ oz (100 g) pieces and shape each into a ball. Let rise for 20 minutes, then shape into long, thin loaves, 4 in (10 cm) in length. Brush the loaves with egg wash and roll them in very fine wheat semolina. Chill in the refrigerator for 15 minutes. Using a sharp knife, cut parallel slashes at an angle in the top of each loaf, then put them in a proving cabinet at 77 °F (25 °C) and let rise for 1 hour 30 minutes.

Preheat the oven to 340 °F (170 °C/ Gas Mark 3) on steam setting and bake the loaves for 16 minutes. After removing them from the oven, let the loaves cool on a wire rack.

Raoul Maeder

Artisan baker at Le Pain d'Exclamation and President of the Jury of the Coupe de France des Écoles

In 2016 I co-developed with Maison Weiss the Sublime range of chocolate for making bread, Viennese pastries, and sponge cakes. We were seeking to create a chocolate that could be baked in the oven without any deterioration of its flavor and texture. The development of Sublime dark chocolate took eight months; after which came Sublime milk chocolate.

Chocolate
KUGELHOPF

SERVES 6

Preparation time : 1 hour
Kneading time : 30 minutes
Rising and resting time :
3 hours 30 minutes
Cooking time : 45 minutes

2 1 lb 5 oz (600 g) kugelhopf molds,
preferably terracotta

Poolish (for pre-fermentation)
1 ⅔ cups (5 ¼ oz/150 g)
cake flour (T45)
⅔ cup (150 ml) milk, well chilled
1/10 oz (0.3 g) fresh yeast

Kugelhopfs
1 ⅓ oz (37.5 g) fresh yeast
1 tablespoon + 2 teaspoons
(25 ml) skim milk, well chilled +
1 tablespoon + 2 teaspoons (25 ml)
for bassinage
5 ½ cups (1 lb 2 oz/500 g)
cake flour (T45)
Scant ½ cup (3 oz/82.5 g)
superfine sugar
2 teaspoons (10 g) fine salt
5 ¼ oz (150 g) free-range whole egg
(about 3 eggs), well chilled
1 ½ teaspoons (10 g)
Diamalt or honey
7 oz (200 g) softened butter
5 oz (145 g) Weiss Sublime dark
chocolate + 5 oz (145 g) Weiss
Sublime milk chocolate, stored at
least overnight in the refrigerator

For the molds
Butter for greasing
Whole raw almonds

Preparing the poolish

Stir the flour and a little of the milk together until smooth. Stir this mixture together with the remaining milk and the yeast in a mixing bowl. Cover and let rest for 2 hours at room temperature.

Preparing the kugelhopfs

In the bowl of a stand mixer fitted with the dough hook, crumble the yeast into a little of the first quantity of milk. Add the flour, poolish, sugar, salt, yeast mixture, remaining milk, eggs, and Diamalt or honey and begin kneading everything together, taking care not to let the dough get too warm. At the end of the kneading, the temperature of it should be between 75 and 79 °F (24 and 26 °C).

Work the ingredients together on speed 1 for 10 minutes, then increase to speed 2, and continue to knead for an additional 15 minutes. The dough must become smooth. Next work in the softened butter until incorporated. Check the texture of the dough and, if it is too firm, add a little milk (bassinage) to correct the consistency. The dough needs to be shiny and smooth.

Quickly add the dark and milk Sublime chocolates to the dough, then stop kneading. Let the dough rest for 45 minutes, then cut it into 1 lb 2 oz (500 g) pieces and shape each into a ball. Let rise for a further 45 minutes.

Preparing the molds

Butter the kugelhopf molds and arrange the almonds like flower petals in the bottom of each mold.

Baking the kugelhopfs

Press the dough pieces (squeeze them lightly with your hand) and carefully mark a hole in the center of each with your elbow to shape into a crown. Place the crowns in the molds and let rise for 1 hour 30 minutes in a humid atmosphere at 77 °F (25 °C).

Preheat the oven to 325 °F (165 °C/ Gas Mark 3). Place the kugelhopfs in the oven and lower the temperature to 300 °F (155 °C/Gas Mark 2). Bake for 45 minutes, then immediately remove the kugelhopfs from the oven. Let cool on a wire rack.

Gianduja is a classic and the gianduja made by Weiss particularly highlights its intensity, length in the mouth, and creaminess. The combination of gianduja and brioche is one of immense indulgence.

Gianduja

BRIOCHE

SERVES 6

Preparation time :
1 hour 30 minutes
Chilling time : about 18 hours
(rising of the dough) + 30 minutes
Cooking time : 9 minutes

6 small half-sphere silicone molds
about ¾ in–1 ¼ in (2–3 cm)
in diameter

3 ½ oz (100 g) Weiss gianduja
7 cups (1 lb 6 oz/625 g) cake flour
(French croissant and brioche
flour T45)
⅓ cup (2 ¾ oz/75 g) superfine sugar
2 ¼ teaspoons (12.5 g) salt
1 lb ¾ oz (470 g) whole egg
(9 or 10 eggs according to their size)
¾ oz (21 g) fresh yeast
13 oz (375 g) softened butter
1 egg beaten with a few drops
of milk for the egg wash

The dough and the gianduja inserts must be prepared the day before the brioches are cooked.

Melt the gianduja and fill the small half-sphere molds with it. Freeze until the next day. Weigh out the flour, sugar, and salt and keep them in the refrigerator for 30 minutes.

In a stand mixer fitted with the dough hook, knead the flour, salt, sugar, eggs, and crumbled yeast together until the dough leaves the sides of the mixer bowl completely and forms a ball around the dough hook (be warned, this takes time!). Add the softened butter in three equal amounts, kneading constantly until it has been completely incorporated. Wrap the ball of dough in plastic wrap and chill for about 4 hours in the refrigerator.

Take the dough out of the refrigerator, fold it over with your hand, wrap it again in plastic wrap, and chill in the refrigerator until the next day.

On the day of baking, cut the brioche dough into 2 ½-oz (70-g) pieces. Shape each piece into a ball around a small frozen gianduja insert. Let rise for 3 hours in a warm place, then glaze the brioches by brushing the beaten egg over them. Bake in a 325 °F (160 °C/ Gas Mark 3) oven for 8–9 minutes, watching to ensure the brioches do not brown too much.

The ganache used to fill this flaky brioche needed to be made with a powerful chocolate to complement the chocolate-flavored dough. Ébène dark couverture chocolate seemed to me the perfect choice.

Flaky
CHOCOLATE BRIOCHE

SERVES 6

Preparation time :
1 hour 30 minutes
Rising and resting time : 5 hours
Cooking time : 24 minutes

6 stainless steel baking rings,
2 ½ in (6 cm) deep and 3 in (8 cm)
in diameter

Brioches

5 ⅓ cups (1 lb 1 oz/480 g)
cake flour (T45)
3 tablespoons (⅔ oz/20 g) Weiss
cocoa powder
⅓ cup (1 ¾ oz/50 g)
muscovado sugar
5 ¼ oz (150 g) whole egg
(about 3 eggs)
1 ¾ oz (50 g) softened butter
2 teaspoons (10 g) fleur de sel
⅔ oz (20 g) fresh yeast
⅔ cup (150 ml) milk, at room
temperature
10 ½ oz (300 g) laminating butter
with a minimum butterfat content
of 84 %

Egg wash

1 egg yolk
1 teaspoon (5 ml) milk
Brown sugar, for dusting

Rich chocolate ganache

3 oz (75 g) Weiss Ébène 72 %
dark chocolate
6 tablespoons (90 ml)
whipping cream
½ oz (15 g) glucose syrup
½ oz (15 g) honey
⅓ oz (10 g) butter

Preparing the brioches

Place the flour, cocoa powder, muscovado sugar, eggs, the softened butter, and fleur de sel in the bowl of a stand mixer fitted with the dough hook. Crumble the yeast into the milk to liquify it, then add to the mixer bowl with the motor running. Knead until the dough comes away completely from the sides of the mixer bowl (the temperature of the dough must reach 73 °F/23 °C).

Gather the dough into a ball, place it in a bowl, cover the surface with plastic wrap, and let rise for 1 hour 30 minutes at room temperature. At the end of this time, the dough must have doubled in volume. Knead it briefly to burst air bubbles inside it, shape the dough into a rectangle, and freeze for 30 minutes.

Flatten the laminating butter into a square the same size as one short side of the rectangle of dough. Remove the dough from the freezer, place the laminating butter in the center and wrap the dough around it, sealing the edges of the dough. Give the dough a double turn by rolling it into a long rectangle, folding the bottom third up and the top third down so the edges join, then a single turn by rolling the dough again into a rectangle and folding in three like a wallet. Chill for 1 hour.

Roll the dough to a rectangle 12 in (30 cm) wide and ¹⁄₁₆ in (2 mm) thick. Roll up from the top as tightly as possible and cut into 1 ½-in (4-cm) slices. Butter the baking rings and place the dough inside.

Preparing the egg wash and baking the brioches

Make the egg wash by mixing the egg yolk and milk together and brushing it over the brioches. Dust them with brown sugar and let rise for 2 hours. Brush the brioches again with egg wash and bake in a preheated 325 °F (160 °C/Gas Mark 3) oven for 24 minutes. Unmold the brioches and let cool on a wire rack.

Preparing the rich chocolate ganache

Melt the chocolate. Bring the cream, glucose syrup, and honey to a boil and pour over the melted chocolate. Add the butter and blend using a hand-held blender. Chill in the refrigerator for 1 hour, then transfer the ganache to a pastry bag fitted with a long piping tip.

Finishing

Fill the base of the brioches with ganache using the pastry bag, allowing about 1 oz (30 g) for each one.

THE
Renowned
Chefs

Agnès and Pierre

Chefs and proprietors of the Chocolaterie
Agnès et Pierre, Rodez

Agnès and Pierre met while they were training to
become chocolatiers in Toulouse. If Pierre has always
been a pastry chef, Agnès initially chose to study
history, but the appeal of chocolate proved stronger.
As she explains : "It is a great material to work
with and one that has a fascinating history."
Passionately creative and specializing in elegant,
beautifully refined chocolate candies, macarons,
and ice cream, they opened their own chocolate-
making business in Rodez in 2013 and have
a shop at 5, place de la Cité, plus a 400-m² atelier
outside the city.

Loïc and Cédric Beziat

Chefs and proprietors of the Beziat Frères
Pâtisserie, Cahors

Their parents were bakers at Gramat and
now sons Loïc and Cédric are continuing the family
tradition at Cahors under the name of Beziat Frères.
While Cédric focuses more on baking bread,
Loïc is a true pastry chef. After being named
Best Apprentice in France in 2012, Loïc trained
professionals at the ENSP in Yssingeaux, before taking
over as head of the Pâtisserie Canet in Nice.
In 2018 he was voted Best Sugar Artist in the World.
Today, the two brothers combine their expertise
and are synonymous with excellence in
the Cadurcian city.

Sébastien Bras

Chef at the restaurants Le Suquet, Laguiole, and La Halle aux Grains, Paris

In charge of Le Suquet restaurant at Laguiole since 2009, Sébastien Bras is charting his own course on the Aubrac plateau, while still employing the same passion and sensitivity as his father, Michel. He offers a perceptive and carefully crafted cuisine that is perfectly in tune with nature. Among the other restaurants in the Maison Bras stable are L'Espace Gourmand at L'Aire du Viaduc, Millau, and La Halle aux Grains, which recently opened in the Bourse de Commerce (Commodities Exchange) in Paris. In 2021, *Le Coulant au Chocolat* (molten chocolate pudding), created by Michel Bras, celebrated its fortieth anniversary.

Baptiste Brichon

Pastry chef and proprietor of the BAPT Pâtisserie in Macao, China

Baptiste began his baking apprenticeship at the age of 15 in a boulangerie at Angers. He went on to work at Sketch, Pierre Gagnaire's London restaurant, before heading to Australia where he opened a French pâtisserie. In 2013, he settled in Macao, helping to set up the Cacao Pâtisserie boutique, where he remained until 2017, the year he opened his BAPT pâtisserie with his wife, Rene. Taking inspiration from his time as an apprentice and from his travels, his recipes are firmly rooted in the local culture.

Patrice Cabannes

Executive pastry chef at the Atlantis Hotel
in Dubai, UAE

After having gained his Pâtisserie Diploma in Paris,
Patrice Cabannes began an international career,
first in the United States, where he remained for
several years, and then at the Peninsula Hotel in
Bangkok. Since 2014, he has been Executive Pastry
Chef at the Atlantis Hotel, The Palm, in Dubai,
in charge of a team which is responsible for baking
hundreds of exquisite cakes, as well as thousands of
loaves of bread and croissants every day. In 2013,
Pro Magazine named him Dubai's Best Pastry Chef and,
in 2016, he won the title of Pastry Chef of the Year
at The Caterer Middle East Awards.

Jonathan Chauve

Pastry chef and Master Chocolatier at Weiss

After a career as a pastry chef, notably at the Chardon
Bleu in Saint-Just-Saint-Rambert, where he was named
best apprentice in the Loire in 2007, Jonathan joined
the team of teachers at the ENSP-École Ducasse.
Creative and inquiring, he loves to communicate
his passion for the art of making pastries, ice cream,
and chocolate. At Weiss, he effortlessly takes on
the twofold challenge of passing on his knowledge to
the company's clients around the world and bringing
his expertise and ingenuity to the creation of
new recipes for Weiss chocolate and praline.

Marie Dieudonné

Pastry chef and proprietor of Sucré Cœur, Paris

After serving her apprenticeship at Fouquet's in Paris and spending three years working with Laurent Duchêne, Marie Dieudonné opened Sucré Cœur in Paris's 9th arrondissement, close to the rue des Martyrs. Without turning her back on classical techniques, her approach is first and foremost one of creativity, producing pâtisserie that is indulgent, fresh, elegant, and includes a wide choice of gluten-free or vegan items. Everything is made daily on the premises (her development kitchen adjoins the store window). The produce she uses is fresh, organically sourced wherever possible, and respects the cycle of the seasons.

Grégory Doyen

Travelling pâtissier and consultant to GD Sweet Concept

Originally from Burgundy, Gregory has immersed himself in art and pâtisserie since he was a child. Trained in the great French pâtisserie schools of Le Castel at Dijon and the ENSP at Yssingeaux, after graduating he had a three-year internship at Maison Lafay, Lyon. After a spell as a confectioner at the Grand Véfour in Paris, he embarked on an international career which took him to Russia and Taiwan, among other places. In 2018, Gregory set up GD Sweet Concept, a consulting and pâtisserie creation company which involves him travelling the world, moving from one project to another.

François Gagnaire

Chef and proprietor of Anicia restaurant, Paris

Born in the Haute-Loire, François Gagnaire trained at the École Hôtelière de Saint-Chély-d'Apcher in Lozère, before completing his apprenticeship alongside chefs such as Alain Chapel, Pierre Gagnaire, and Guy Lassausaie. He then opened a fine-dining restaurant at the Hôtel du Parc in Puy-en-Velay with his wife Isabelle where, in 2006, he received a Michelin star and, in 2009, was awarded the title of Chevalier de la Médaille de l'Ordre National du Mérite. He is currently chef-proprietor of the Anicia restaurant in the rue du Cherche-Midi in Paris, where he serves dishes made from the finest seasonal ingredients.

Marion Goettlé

Chef and proprietor of the Café Mirabelle, Paris

Marion was born in Strasburg and comes from a long line of restaurateurs. She worked in some of the greatest fine-dining establishments before opening the Café Mirabelle in Paris's 9th arrondissement. She has dedicated the Café to showcasing the pâtisserie and the cuisine of her native Alsace, skilfully updating recipes to suit modern tastes. Viennoiseries and kugelhopf take pride of place, as well as brioches and pastries made with quetsche or mirabelle plums. "It helps to make me feel at home and is a way of sharing my roots with other people," she says.

Jeffery Koo

Executive pastry chef of A Little Sweet
in Manchester, UK

Jeffery Koo Ka Chun is a collector of awards for
pâtisserie, confectionery, and chocolate making.
Known for his extravagant style and his mastery of
chocolate decorations, he has been Assistant Executive
Pastry Chef for the Mandarin Oriental hotel chain
and for chef Pierre Gagnaire in France. He has a very
high profile all over East Asia and between 2015
and 2019 ran his own pâtisserie in Hong Kong.
Since 2021, he has been in charge at A Little Sweet,
the pâtisserie he established in Manchester.

Kevin Lacote

Pastry chef and proprietor of KL Pâtisserie, Paris

Kevin Lacote learned the tools of his trade at
Le Cinq restaurant in the Hotel George V in Paris.
His rise continued at L'Ambroisie, La Grande Cascade,
Hugo & Victor, and he then became Yannick Alléno's
Executive Pastry Chef at The One & Only hotel in
Dubai. This experience enabled him to open his own
establishment, KL Pâtisserie, in 2006 and to teach
pâtisserie courses in his atelier. *Gault & Millau and
L'Express Magazine* in 2017, followed by *Pudlo Paris*
in 2018, awarded him, in rapid succession, the accolade
of Pastry Chef of the Year. He is a member of
the Collège Culinaire de France.

Clément Le Déoré

Pastry chef and proprietor of Desserts By Clément in San Diego, United States

This 30-year-old chef first trained in bread making, then in pâtisserie, before finally deciding to pursue the latter and working as a pastry chef in Corsica for four years. At the end of that time another destination awaited him—Sydney —where he worked in a French pâtisserie for two years. However, his dream had always been to live in the United States, and in 2017 he moved to San Diego. After four years, he had established his own company, Desserts By Clément, and plans to open a boutique at the end of 2022.

Raoul Maeder

Artisan baker at Le Pain d'Exclamation and President of the Jury of the Coupe de France des Écoles

At the Boulangerie-Pâtisserie Maeder, bread and pastry making has passed from father to son since 1956. Bread making is a family tradition that has been handed down from generation to generation, along with the secrets of the finest recipes from Alsace. Before being trained by his father at the boulangerie, Raoul served his apprenticeship in the most prestigious establishments. Since then, he has won his first awards, as much for the originality of his creations as their quality, and he exports his knowledge overseas as a consultant. In 2016 he was the co-creator, with Weiss, of their Sublime chocolate chips.

Régis Marcon

Chef at the Maisons Marcon, Saint-Bonnet-le-Froid

Master chef Régis Marcon is originally from Saint-Bonnet-le-Froid, and he has remained faithful to his region and his village, where he and his son, Jacques, run Le Clos des Cimes (which has held three Michelin stars since 2005). They also have several other restaurants and a pâtisserie, all of which are named after mushrooms. His affinity for solving puzzles is well known and it led him to creating Chococèpes in 2017 with Weiss, a couverture chocolate with ceps. Built on confidence and loyalty, his collaboration with Weiss has endured for four decades.

Morgane Raimbaud

Pastry chef at the Alliance restaurant, Paris

Twice voted Dessert Champion of France (she won the Junior title in 2016 and the Professional title in 2020), Morgane Raimbaud followed her initial cookery training with an apprenticeship in pâtisserie, a discipline in which she is one of today's rising stars. Her time spent working in Michelin-starred fine-dining restaurants, including the Plaza Athénée, Taillevent, and Shangri-La, enabled her to acquire a real technical mastery. The elegance and delicacy of her creations does not exclude her willingness to take bold risks and Morgane never hesitates to introduce unexpected flavors such as peppercorns, spices, or different olive oils into her desserts.

Johanna Roques

Pastry chef and proprietor of Jojo & Co, Paris

The move from Canal +, where she worked for twenty years, to pâtisserie, heralded Johanna Roques' decision to turn her passion into her career. In 2002, she began studying bread making and pâtisserie, and this led to her creating her own brand, Jojo & Co. First she opened La Pâtisserie du Marché in the Place d'Aligre, Paris, and then, in 2018, Jojo & Co Bourdaloue, close to the church of Notre-Dame-de-Lorette. Her top priorities are seasonality, the quality of raw ingredients, and the traceability of the products she uses for her creations that are made 100 % in house.

Christophe Roure

Chef and proprietor
of Le Neuvième Art restaurant, Lyon

Born at Craponne-sur-Arzon, Christophe Roure is the complete chef, having mastered every discipline in the restaurant repertoire. Trained in cooking, charcuterie, and pâtisserie, this Meilleur Ouvrier de France (cooking category) has worked for, among others, La Poularde, Pierre Gagnaire at Saint-Étienne, and Régis Marcon at Saint-Bonnet-le-Froid. He is the chef-proprietor of Le Neuvième Art restaurant in Lyon, which holds two Michelin stars.

Hari Unterrainer

Executive pastry chef of the Crown Resorts Chain in Melbourne, Australia

Born at Lienz, in Austria, Harald Unterrainer made his first cake at the age of 13 for his brother's birthday. Once he discovered his ability to make people happy by baking them a cake, his destiny was assured. He began as a confectioner in Lienz, but soon took off to work as a pastry chef in numerous luxury hotels around the world. This great traveler is very in tune with the changing demands of his clientele (such as vegetarianism and the importance of sourcing ingredients locally) and has been Executive Pastry Chef of the Crown Resorts Chain in Melbourne since 2015.

ACKNOWLEDGMENTS

Founded in 1882 and still rooted in Saint-Étienne, the Maison Weiss is one of the oldest established chocolate makers in France. For 140 years now, Weiss has led the way in chocolate innovations that keep traditions alive, displaying a treasure-trove of craft skills that in 2014 won the *Entreprise du Patrimoine Vivant* label.

Special thanks go to all those people whose efforts over the years have turned chocolate and praline-making into an art – generations of talented individuals working like cellar mistresses and cellar masters to create daring symphonies of flavor.

Thanks also to our 130 partners, all of them dedicated to the uncompromising quality of chocolate with a unique taste and reputation that we are proud to call Weiss.

Thank you to all those people who take our passion to a higher level – chefs, pastry chefs, bakers, cooks, culinary alchemists and other inventors of sweet indulgences. Thank you for pushing back the boundaries of chocolate creativity. Thank you for making us proud to face the future, working hand in hand with you to ensure the success of our next-generation couverture chocolate, chocolate products and pralines.

Thank you to all those artists – street artists, poets and illustrators – who have nurtured our artist-cum-artisan soul since the beginning.

Thank you to our cooperative partners for sharing our commitment to sustainable gastronomy, all the way from the cocoa pod and the bean to the finished chocolate.

To all of those passionate people who have supported and inspired Weiss for more than 140 years: THANK YOU!

Graphic design and production: Laurence Maillet

Publishing: Virginie Mahieux and Pauline Dubuisson

Texts: Claire Pichon
Coordination of the Chefs' collective and rewriting
of the recipes: Sophie Brissaud

Photographs: Matthieu Cellard
Styling: Garlone Bardel

Translation from French to English: Florence Brutton
Translation of the recipes: Wendy Sweetser
Proofreading: Nicole Foster

ABRAMS
The Art of Books

Photoengraver: Quadrilaser
Printed in Portugal
Legal Deposit : october 2022
ISBN : 978-1-4197-6748-7